Prince Estabrook
slave and soldier

by Alice M. Hinkle

Pleasant Mountain Press
PMB 403
405 Waltham Street
Lexington, Mass. 02421-7934

Printed in USA, Kirkwood Printing, Wilmington, Mass.

ISBN 0-9679771-0-X
Library of Congress Control Number: 2001130094

Cover photo: *Charles H. Price Jr., reenactor and member of
the Lexington Minute Men, dashes from Buckman Tavern
toward Lexington Green*, Copyright ©2001 by Ann Ringwood

Drawing, photographs, and map by Jan van Steenwijk,
Copyright ©2001 by Jan van Steenwijk

Cover, book design, and graphics by Jan van Steenwijk
Production and editorial assistance by Jeanette Webb

Table of Contents

This book is dedicated to the memory
of Prince Estabrook and the thousands
of other courageous black patriots
long denied the recognition they deserve.

*From the earliest days of our nation, African Americans answered the call to arms
in defense of America whenever that call came. From our Revolution to our Civil
War, black men and women on the battlefield were crucial to victory.*

*Yet the fame and fortune that were their just due in return for blood spent,
lives lost, and battles won, was never waiting for them when the wars ended.*

—from a speech by Colin L. Powell, then chairman, U.S. Joint Chiefs of Staff,
in Ft. Leavenworth, Kans., at the dedication of the Buffalo Soldier Monument, July 25, 1992

Introduction

My fascination with the American Revolution began decades ago when I was growing up in Dayton, Ohio. I cheered the fight for liberty and the courage of Paul Revere, George Washington, Patrick Henry, and other heroes. But it wasn't until I moved to Lexington, Mass., and discovered Prince Estabrook and the black patriots that I realized there was an even more poignant story tied to the colonists' gallant quest for freedom. It took my breath away.

Charles H. Price Jr., past commander of the Lexington Minute Men, introduced me to Prince Estabrook in 1987 when I interviewed Price for a newspaper article. For more than 20 years he has played the role of slave and soldier Prince Estabrook in Patriot's Day[1] reenactments of the clash that launched the Revolutionary War.

Although I was amazed that Lexington's militia company had included a slave, there wasn't much information on Prince Estabrook. I finished my article quickly, but I couldn't shake a growing excitement about the man who seemed to have slipped between the cracks of history. In December 1994, with the support of a Lexington Council for the Arts grant, I set out to discover just who Prince Estabrook was.

Nearly seven years later, after visiting sites, digging through archives, and following leads, I've encountered misinformation, dead ends, and a tantalizing mix of fact and legend. Long discussions with Price added passion and heart to the story and helped me to see Estabrook as a person as well as a soldier.

While the puzzle of Prince Estabrook is still riddled with missing pieces, what I did find indicates that Estabrook was both courageous and kind. As my search continued, I also came to understand how this black man could have become virtually invisible during one of the defining events in American history. The reason is tied to slavery and a heritage of discrimination that stubbornly lingers centuries later.

There is still much to discover, but I believe that it is important for a wider audience to meet Prince Estabrook and to understand how, through circumstance and destiny, he became the first black soldier[2] in the American Revolution at dawn on April 19, 1775. His blood was among the first shed in America's defense that day. Estabrook and other black patriots played an important role in the War for Independence. It is time to honor their efforts.

It is my hope that this story of Prince Estabrook, more outline than portrait, will be the catalyst for more inquiries into his life and into the way we look at the Revolution and perhaps ourselves.

Alice M. Hinkle
April 2001

Keeping the story alive

Glowing lantern light spills out of the windows of Buckman Tavern in Lexington, Mass., during the first hours of this modern-day April morning. Eerie ripples of light and shadow dart past the pale yellow clapboards, glance off the brick walkway, then dissolve in darkness.

Inside, men dressed in the rugged garb of colonial farmers and tradesmen huddle in the taproom, muskets at their sides. Outside, other members of today's Lexington Minute Men[1] shiver in the predawn chill, conferring anxiously on the tavern grounds and on the town common across the road.

Closer to daybreak thousands of people crowd four and five deep around the common, or Battle Green, where reenactors will bring to life the encounter that occurred here April 19, 1775. Children perch on their parents' shoulders. Some cling to ladders and trees. Others wriggle closer to the roped-off area. Veteran Patriot's Day battle watchers are easy to spot. They come equipped with binoculars, blankets, cameras, and folding chairs.

Although there will be no surprises in this performance, the mood is somber. Messengers playing the roles of Paul Revere and William Dawes have already spread the word that British Regulars are headed to Lexington, on their way to destroy stashes of gunpowder, cannon, and other military supplies in Concord. After mustering earlier, members of Lexington's training band[2] who live nearby have returned home to grab some sleep and listen for the belfry bell that could call them back.

The air is thick with an unsettling mix of tension, fear, and excitement. Shafts of light break through the sky as militia scout Thaddeus Bowman, played by Norman Daigle, rides up to the tavern on horseback and calls frantically for Captain John Parker.

Parker, played by George Gabriel,[3] rushes out, and Bowman shouts the news: the Regulars are approaching—fast. Parker directs three men to fire muskets into the air and orders young drummer William Diamond, played by Stephen Cole, to begin the throbbing call to arms. The belfry bell rings out its urgent alarm.

Seconds later Charles H. Price Jr., a tall African American who portrays the slave Prince Estabrook, is among the militiamen who stream across the road from Buckman Tavern. Amid the noise and confusion he joins the ranks, then answers the company roll call.

The drumbeat quickens. Footsteps pound in the distance, and flashes of scarlet uniforms come into focus. It is clear His Majesty's soldiers are on a mission that spells danger for the militiamen who wait nervously on the common. As Estabrook strains to hear, Parker barks out the instructions that later became legend and are carved in stone on the Battle Green: *Stand your ground. Don't fire unless fired upon; but if they mean to have war, let it begin here.*[4]

Charles Price, center, and other Lexington Minute Men stand ready as the Redcoats approach.

Members of the modern-day British 10th Regiment of Foot and Lexington Minute Men in a Patriot's Day reenactment

Soon wave upon wave of Regulars file onto the common, facing the armed colonists. Major John Pitcairn of the Royal Marines, played by a reenactor from the British 10th Regiment of Foot, addresses the rebels. "Lay down your arms, disperse, and go home," he commands. One Lexington man cries out, "You won't get my gun."

Pitcairn directs his troops to round up the rebels and take their weapons. With muskets and bayonets pointing at the outnumbered Lexington militia, a British lieutenant commands, "Slow march." Parker tells his troops, "Fall back and give way." They take a few steps back. Suddenly a mysterious shot rings out, followed by volleys of musket fire. Estabrook clutches his left shoulder, then falls to the ground.

During the exchange, Jonas Parker, played by James Hart, is also among those hit. Reeling from his wound, he tries desperately to reload. As he struggles, a British soldier aims a flashing bayonet at Parker's chest and strikes him. Parker, a cousin of the American captain, slumps, drops, then is still. Another member of the Lexington company, Jonathan Harrington, played by Jeffrey Long, is mortally wounded. He slowly crawls to the steps of his home just beyond the common and takes his last breaths in the arms of his wife.

In minutes the firing slows and stops. Billows of smoke clear, but the bitter odor lingers. The Regulars regroup and fire a volley in honor of King George. Then with fife and drum blaring, they march resolutely off to Concord where there will be another deadly confrontation at the North Bridge.

The Lexington militia takes stock of its casualties, which include eight dead, seven from Parker's company. One of the eight fatalities is Woburn resident Asahel Porter, whom the British had earlier taken prisoner on the road to Lexington.

The eloquent, fiery First Parish pastor Jonas Clarke, played by Hancock United Church of Christ minister Peter Meek, begins moving the dead to the side of the common. Others hurry to assist the nine wounded, including Estabrook.

The sky brightens, the crowd disperses, and the reenactment of this bloody encounter is over for another year. But for the members of Captain Parker's company who put their lives on the line more than 225 years ago, the end of that morning's bloodshed was the beginning of a long, painful fight for their country's independence. For Estabrook, it was also the start of a personal journey from slavery to freedom.

Looking back

$\mathfrak{I}$magine the media blitz if the events that unfolded on April 19, 1775, were to occur today. TV camera crews and reporters from around the globe would swoop down on Lexington and Concord, anxious to find eyewitnesses to share their stories. Prince Estabrook, as the only slave to participate in the day's first clash of arms, might well have become an instant celebrity.

Instead, in 1775, news was spread by word of mouth and by express riders, or it was printed in a few crude newspapers or broadsides

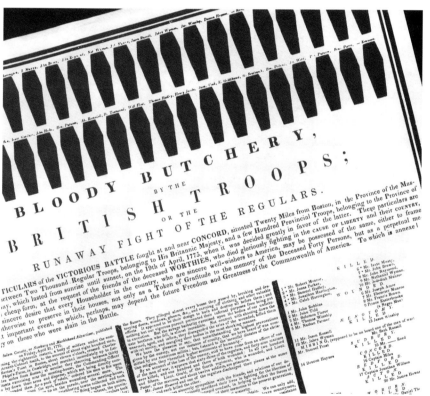

This "Bloody Butchery" broadside shows Prince Estabrook's name, followed by the words "A Negro man" in the list of those wounded April 19, 1775.

(one-page accounts tacked to trees and tavern walls). One famous broadside, circulating soon after April 19, helped further fan the flames of the colonists' resentment and their hunger for liberty. Headlined "Bloody Butchery by the British Troops," it gives the Provincial Congress's official account of the Battle of Lexington and Concord. The publication, which lists Prince Estabrook among the wounded, features a chilling illustration of a double row of black coffins, each box representing a colonist killed by the King's forces.

While many members of Captain Parker's company gave depositions or wrote about the part they played in the events that morning, Estabrook left no personal account. Nor did fellow soldiers or onlookers bother to describe his role, other than to note his injury.

According to tradition, Estabrook joined the Lexington militia as early as 1773, but records that could have confirmed this have disappeared, as have many other important Lexington documents from the spring of 1775.[1]

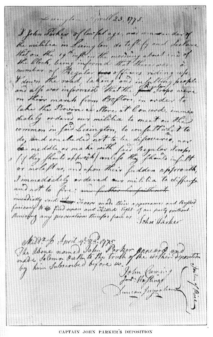

CAPTAIN JOHN PARKER'S DEPOSITION

Captain John Parker's 1775 deposition

Without much in the way of written record, one is forced to speculate about why Estabrook was fighting in the first place. Prince had accompanied his master, Benjamin Estabrook, and other Lexington soldiers on earlier expeditions, so his experience may have been valued by the militia. He may have been serving because of a sense of duty or loyalty to Benjamin. It's also possible that he was taking Benjamin's place, or perhaps hoping that his efforts would help him to gain his own freedom from slavery.

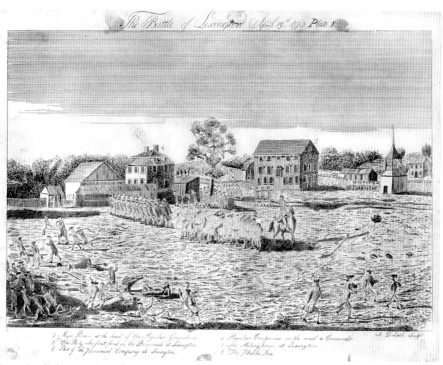

Amos Doolittle engraving of the April 19, 1775, encounter at Lexington, based on sketches by Ralph Earl

Whatever the reason he was there, it's probably safe to say that along with the others who did speak out, Prince Estabrook was confused and frightened as the crimson swath of British troops advanced.

April 18, 1775, had been a damp and raw day, but the sky cleared as darkness arrived. By midnight, moonlight bathed the countryside in a milky glow.

The Lexington company's membership numbered between 120 and 140 men. Seventy to 77 militiamen were milling around the common and tavern area when the Redcoats arrived about 5 a.m. on April 19.[2] The identity of the person who fired the first shot remains a mystery. Some theories attribute it to one of the estimated 700 British Regulars. Others claim it was fired by a colonist, perhaps one of the bystanders near the tavern. There are also differing descriptions of the battle and the resistance mounted by the Lexington militia.

A print created from the Amos Doolittle engraving more than 60 years after April 19, 1775

Woodcut of Concord's North Bridge, April 19, 1775

Early reports indicated little if any colonial return of fire on Lexington Green. Many described a massacre. Engravings, said to be based on eyewitness accounts, show local militia fleeing a brutal, unprovoked attack. Such an interpretation, however, would have been the one most likely to fuel patriotic sentiments and the will to strike back.[3]

Later testimony from a series of Lexington militiamen describes limited return of fire, although not enough to constitute a "battle." That version of events is backed up by reports of at least one British injury and a British horse being grazed by a musket ball.[4] One of the later accounts was given by Joseph Estabrook IV, Benjamin's eldest son.[5]

After marching off Lexington common on April 19, 1775, the Redcoats continued toward Concord for an encounter that would make it clear that the rebels were organized and determined to fight for their rights. Four of the seven British Light Infantry companies sent to the North Bridge continued to Barrett's farm beyond the North Bridge to search for supplies. Three companies (about 95 men) remained to protect the bridge and retreated to the town center after the skirmish.[6]

Joseph Paquette's depiction of the April 19, 1775, action at the "Bloody Angle" shows British soldiers along the Battle Road.

Meanwhile, even before word had spread about the casualties in Lexington, minutemen and militia began to respond from near and far. The colonials, gathering above the bridge, fearful that the town of Concord was being burned by the British, marched to protect it. The Acton company led the way to the North Bridge, with Captain Isaac Davis out in front, joined by Concord's Major John Buttrick and Westford's Lieutenant Colonel John Robinson of Prescott's regiment.

The encounter at the bridge was brief and deadly. It forced the Regulars to withdraw and retreat to the town center. Three British soldiers were killed and eight wounded, including four officers. For the colonials, two were killed, including Davis, and four were wounded.[7] By midday the pivotal running battle of the British Retreat had begun along a narrow corridor that stretched 16 miles from Meriam's Corner in Concord all the way to Charlestown.

Thousands of militia and minutemen from more than 25 communities converged on the exhausted Regulars as they tried to leave Concord. Although the British soldiers probably thought that their situation couldn't get much worse, they still faced the fiercest fighting of the day, clashes that would leave political and social wounds impossible to heal.[8]

Peter Salem crouches as he fires a musket from behind a tree.

Prince Estabrook was sidelined by his wound, but Captain Parker and his company met the Regulars again during the afternoon of April 19. Other black patriots who joined in the fighting included Pomp Blackman of Lexington, Caesar Bason of Westford, Cato Wood and Cuff Whittemore of Menotomy, Peter Salem of Framingham,[9] and Cato Bordman and Cato Stedman of Cambridge.[10]

As the fight moved into Lincoln and back to Lexington, militiamen continued to swell the rebel ranks. Familiar with the terrain, they surprised the Redcoats by shooting from behind stone walls and trees. They also used more conventional military formations and skills picked up during regular training sessions.

When the ragged British troops returned to Lexington shortly after 2 p.m., they found about 1,000 welcome reinforcements commanded by Lord Hugh Percy. Taking over Munroe Tavern as a temporary hospital, most of the beleaguered troops tended their wounds, rested, and regrouped for the trip back to Charlestown.[11]

The day's bloodiest battle would occur in late afternoon in Menotomy (Arlington). At the Jason Russell farmhouse, visitors can still see and touch the hole left by one of the musketballs flying thick and fast that day. Menotomy is where almost half the day's casualties on both sides occurred. Total colonial losses on April 19 have been estimated at 49 dead, 25 of the deaths occurring in Menotomy. Forty were wounded and five missing. The Regulars' casualties on April 19 numbered 73 dead, 174 wounded, and 26 missing.[12]

Today the series of April 19 clashes, from dawn to dusk, is known collectively as the Battle of Lexington and Concord. Research continues to identify all the soldiers of color who participated that day.[13]

The Jason Russell farmhouse, Arlington.

"When liberty is the prize"

Charles Price, now in his sixties, is no stranger to Patriot's Day celebrations. He grew up in a two-family frame house on Moreland Street in Roxbury, Mass., around the corner from the elegant stone house where patriot and physician Joseph Warren once lived. Price remembers the excitement of the annual April holiday—a parade with crowds, bands, and marchers from the local VFW post. Veterans would pause at a statue of Warren in the nearby square, offering tributes and a rifle salute. Then they would continue to the old burying ground at Washington and Eustis streets for more ceremonies.

The story of America's fight for freedom captured Price's imagination. When he was a teenager, he memorized Warren's words inscribed on a plaque attached to the statue. Price can still recite them today:

> *When liberty is the prize,*
> *Who would shun the warfare?*
> *Who would stoop*
> *to waste a coward thought on life?*[1]

The Warren statue was later moved from the square, stored, then relocated in 1970 to Roxbury Latin School grounds, but the plaque quoting the famous patriot, scholar, and physician was lost.[2]

Price studied the American Revolution in school. He learned that Crispus Attucks, a biracial and runaway slave, was the first of five colonists killed by British soldiers in the 1770 Boston Massacre. But the history books failed to mention that soldiers of color fought in the War for Independence or that they served side by side with their white counterparts.

Charles Price as Estabrook during a practice for a Patriot's Day reenactment

So, when a neighbor asked Price in the mid-1970s, to join the modern day Lexington Minute Men, he was amazed to discover the existence of Prince Estabrook. "Since we all assume the role of one of the original members [in reenactments], I was proud to take the role of Prince Estabrook, and I'm proud to be a [Lexington] Minute Man," Price says.[3]

As a member of the Lexington militia, Estabrook "had to take an oath, vowing to be ready to sacrifice everything dear in life, even life itself, for the common cause. So when the call came, he answered," Price adds.

When he plays the role of Estabrook, Price tries to imagine what the slave may have been thinking on that day in 1775. During the reenactments, Price explains, "you get very much into the role. There's a sense of urgency . . . . We know something momentous is about to happen. When our scout tells us the British are close, the adrenaline starts to pump. You run onto the Green and think, 'This thing is starting to get really out of control.'

"When Captain Parker is exhorting you to stand your ground, you get caught up in the moment. You're staring at the enemy down the barrel of your musket, and you see their muskets and their bayonets flashing. It's scary and very emotional. Even when you know it's just a reenactment, there's this ominous feeling," he says.

Price doesn't believe that Estabrook thought much about the consequences of his actions on that fateful morning. "The British were coming, and I think he was out there with the rest of them, just trying to stay alive," he says.

"Sometimes when I talk to people about what happened in 1775, I try to relate it to something they might know about, such as the 1992 riots in Los Angeles. There was shooting, looting, destruction of property—practically anarchy. Everyone says, 'Yeah, we remember that.' Then I say, 'Remember what happened when they put federal troops in there.' There was

Reproduction of "Dawn of Victory," by Henry Sandham

still tension, but in Los Angeles, when the federal troops went in, everything stopped very quickly," says Price.

Similar dynamics were present in 1775, according to Price. The 1765 Stamp Act, imposing duties on legal documents, dice, newspapers, pamphlets, almanacs, and playing cards, had ignited a powder keg of resentment. Instead of loosening controls on the colonists to ease tensions, British officials piled on new demands, including the 1767 Townshend Acts and the 1773 Tea Act, which led to the Boston Tea Party.

"People were frustrated and angry, storing arms, and guns, and so forth," Price says. "And here come the federal troops. But instead of stopping, these guys back in 1775 didn't back down, and [some of them] fired on the government troops. Can you imagine doing that? It's unbelievable."

Price believes Estabrook may have been aware of the paradox of fighting for the freedom of a country that enslaved him. "It probably at least crossed his mind that everyone was talking about freedom and rights being ignored. He would be risking his life. What would he be fighting for?" Price asks.

But he rejects the idea that race was on the minds of the militia members as the British marched toward them that April morning. "I don't think the men that day were thinking about the color of anyone's skin. They were only thinking about one color, the red of the British soldiers' coats. Those people on the Green in 1775—they were all American heroes," he says.[4]

Price thinks it would have been hard for Estabrook to believe that a black man would ever lead a Lexington militia group, as Price did from 1984 to 1986. "I don't think [Prince Estabrook] could have dreamed of it. It's a little bit beyond my imagination, too, but it happened," Price says.

From farm field to battlefield

Prince Estabrook's story in Lexington begins on December 15, 1691, when the general court granted the petition of Cambridge Farms (later Lexington) residents to establish their own parish. In March of 1693, Reverend Benjamin Estabrook was invited to be its first minister. Eight months later, Benjamin's father, Reverend Joseph Estabrook of Concord, bought 200 acres of land in the Vine Brook area.[1] The congregation built a house for Benjamin and his wife on his father's land, near the site of the current Cary Memorial Building. It contained a hall, south chamber, a best chamber, study, garret, and cellar.[2]

Benjamin did not have long to enjoy his position or home, however, as he died four years later, in 1697. Some of the property's 200 acres changed hands, but by 1699 Benjamin's brother Joseph II owned all but 20 acres of the land originally bought by his father.[3] Joseph II became an important figure in Lexington, serving as clerk, treasurer, assessor, selectman, surveyor, representative to the general court, and teacher at the town's first men's school.[4]

After his death in 1733, Joseph's home and the land around it went to his son Joseph III, who died just seven years later. Joseph III was captain of the local military group, a deacon, and a selectman. His will called for his son Benjamin, then 11, to eventually get the house and 51 acres. Two other sons received larger pieces of the then 300-acre property.[5]

By 1775, Benjamin Estabrook was a distinguished Lexington citizen and one of five slaveholders in the town.[6] He was active in town government and, at various times, served as coroner, town moderator, justice of the peace, and selectman.[7]

In addition to cultivating his own land, Benjamin Estabrook one year received the selectmen's permission to rent the town's "best meadow"[8] to raise more crops. He and his wife, the former Hannah Hubbard, had nine children and a busy life on their sprawling Vine Brook Farm.

The Estabrook property included a mill pond and grist mill operated by the Estabrook and the Loring families. The mill stood at a drop in the Vine Brook near what is now Sheridan Street. It remained active for at least a century, and the pond was used for baptisms in the early 1800s.[9]

How and when Prince arrived in Lexington and became the property of Benjamin Estabrook remains a mystery. Prince Estabrook was about 34 years old at the start of the Revolutionary War.[10] Although there are no records of his birth, he carried the surname of his master. The origin of his first name is unknown. One legend suggests that he was called Prince because his father was African royalty, but there is no evidence to back that claim.[11] "Prince" was among the more common names for male slaves at that time.

In the 1700s, many masters also gave their slaves Greek or Latin first names, such as Pompey, Caesar, and Cato. The names were borrowed from the classics, which were popular with educated white colonists.[12] Today, the irony of choosing such grand names for slaves seems a cruel joke.

According to local tradition, Prince Estabrook was among the many blacks who landed in the Boston area after having been stolen from homes in Africa and sold from the slave ships in Bristol and Newport.[13, 14] But there are problems with that story. There is no record of a notice to selectmen that an unnamed man, boy, or someone named Prince came to live with the Estabrook family. In colonial times, it was customary for residents to inform selectmen when they took in unrelated persons and to describe the newcomers' financial circumstances, for instance "poor" or "good." Selectmen also had the power to order or "warn" persons out of town if they felt the newcomers could become a financial burden for the town.[15]

Minutes of Lexington Board of Selectmen meetings in the 1700s contain long lists of persons who had been warned out of town and residents giving notice of persons arriving—slaves, servants, freemen and women, even babies. But the only notice by Benjamin Estabrook about the arrival of a child or adult male in the years leading up to 1775 is a May 1753 report that Jacob Freeman, formerly of Littleton, had arrived. Jacob's surname suggests that he was a free man, probably hired as a farmhand.[16]

While Prince's arrival may have gone unnoticed, it's also possible that he was the son of Tony, a slave owned by Benjamin Estabrook's grandfather, Joseph II. His will directs that his slave Tony "not be sold" and that he be allowed to choose his master from among Estabrook's children, one of whom was Benjamin's father, Joseph III.[17]

Michael J. Canavan, a turn-of-the-century Boston historian who wrote extensively about Lexington, made numerous references to Tony in unpublished manuscripts in Lexington's Cary Memorial Library collection. A section of Estabrook land that the slave was known to frequent was called Tony pasture or Tony meadow.[18]

A section of Joseph Estabrook II's will

If Prince were the son of Tony, it would explain reports in Estabrook family histories of Benjamin having inherited Prince from his father. It might also explain the apparently close relationship between Benjamin and Prince. Benjamin was older than Prince, but the two may have grown up in the same household. It's possible that as Prince became older, Benjamin came to rely on him for friendship, as well as for help in maintaining the property that was Benjamin's inheritance.

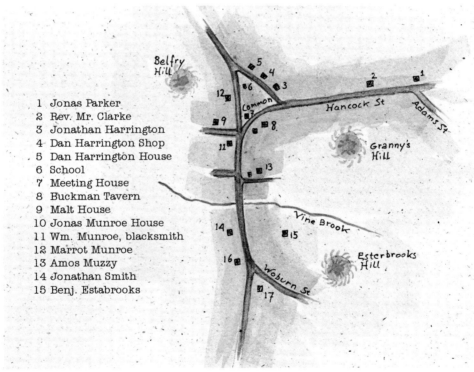

1 Jonas Parker
2 Rev. Mr. Clarke
3 Jonathan Harrington
4 Dan Harrington Shop
5 Dan Harrington House
6 School
7 Meeting House
8 Buckman Tavern
9 Malt House
10 Jonas Munroe House
11 Wm. Munroe, blacksmith
12 Marrot Munroe
13 Amos Muzzy
14 Jonathan Smith
15 Benj. Estabrooks

A Lexington map, circa 1775, shows the site of Esterbrooks [sic] Hill and Benjamin Estabrook's home (15).

Additional evidence of the bonds that linked these two men comes from reports in the Canavan papers. In one case, Canavan describes Benjamin as "a shrewd [horse] trader" who was known to team up with Prince to close a deal. One day, Canavan writes, "Ben was trying to sell a rather poor horse to a back countryman, and Prince was seen walking around with tears in his eyes," urging Benjamin not to sell the animal.[19]

Prince lived with the Estabrook family on land near the edge of the town center, off the main route leading west to Concord and east to Cambridge. The property bordered both sides of the road to Woburn (now Woburn Street). Most of the land lay east of the Vine Brook. A map, circa 1775, shows Esterbrooks [sic] Hill rising northeast of Vine Street, near the spot where it now meets Hayes Lane.

Estabrook family histories report that Joseph IV, Benjamin's oldest son, was on Lexington common with Prince Estabrook on the morning of April 19, 1775. Joseph, then 17, narrowly missed being hit.[20] After the British left for Concord, Joseph helped some of the wounded, including Prince, to the Estabrook home, where they were treated by Dr. Joseph Fiske.[21]

Earlier that day Benjamin Estabrook had moved his wife and younger children to safety, probably to the home of Benjamin Brown. From the Brown farmhouse, the family could catch glimpses of the afternoon action as the weary British soldiers and reinforcements headed back toward Boston, often under fire.[22]

The Estabrook home was one of those visited with fire and destruction by British troops as they retreated. Prince and young Joseph may have surprised the intruders, since the damages that Benjamin sought were among the lowest claims that Lexington property owners submitted for that day's losses.[23]

Dolittle engraving of the fire and destruction that the British showered on Lexington during the retreat

Fighting for liberty . . . and liberation

Prince Estabrook's wound healed following the April 19th encounter, and he was back in action with Captain Parker's Lexington company on June 17 and 18, 1775.[1] The men helped guard the Cambridge headquarters of the newly formed Continental Army as the Battle of Bunker Hill raged in Charlestown, mostly on nearby Breed's Hill.

Prince's master, Benjamin Estabrook, was paid nine pounds for serving five months with a Revolutionary War unit that formed in the summer of 1775. Their mission was to bring back and guard cannon acquired when the Americans captured Fort Ticonderoga in May of 1775.[2]

More than a year passed before the call to arms came again for Prince. Perhaps he was needed in Lexington to help tend crops, or he may have been among the soldiers affected by controversy concerning service by black men, free or enslaved *(for further discussion, see pp. 43–48)*. By July of 1776, Prince was on his way to Fort Ticonderoga, one of 73 privates in Colonel Jonathan Reed's regiment and the company of Captain Charles Miles of Concord. Edmund Munroe of Lexington was named the regiment's 1st lieutenant on July 10 and quartermaster on July 16.[3]

Estabrook and Pompey Blackman were the only African Americans among more than 20 Lexington men in this unit, assembled in response to a Northern Army call for 3,000 soldiers from Massachusetts. The men were needed to help replenish an army drained by battle losses, a smallpox epidemic, and desertions. American leaders were hoping the fresh troops would stabilize the army, which had been forced to retreat from Canada to Crown Point, N.Y., then to Fort Ticonderoga.[4]

After Estabrook's unit assembled, the troops marched to Charlestown, N.H., and headed through the woods along Captain John Stark's route to Fort Ticonderoga. On August 6, Munroe wrote his wife, Rebecca, saying that all the men were in good health and ready to tackle the last leg of the journey that day.[5]

Revolutionary War soldiers confer.

Fort Ticonderoga Museum curator Christopher Fox reports that, by the late 1700s, most of the trees around the fort had been cleared and used for firewood or construction. Even in early fall, chill winds could sweep across the fortress, perched high on a bluff above Lake Champlain. Soldiers' quarters were often nothing more than a simple drafty log hut or possibly a tent. Snow could blanket the wooden and limestone fortifications as early as November.

On October 11, 1776, the American fleet on Lake Champlain was defeated, and nine days later Munroe wrote that the men were bracing for a British attack at any hour. Instead, British General Sir Guy Carleton surprised the Americans by ordering his forces to winter quarters in Canada and abandoning Crown Point on November 3.

While Estabrook and the other troops at Fort Ticonderoga escaped attack, they were kept busy with all the tasks required to operate the fort— cutting wood for campfires, preparing food, doing guard duty, and performing the endless jobs of maintenance and repairs.[6]

"The nights are cold, and it is hard laying on the cold ground," Munroe wrote in a November 13 letter. He added that, with the British at their winter quarters, the company, including Munroe, Estabrook, and the other Lexington men, would soon be heading home.[7]

Records show the unit was discharged November 30. Pay for this trip was authorized February 18, 1777, with the Lexington men earning a penny a mile for the 190 miles they traveled, plus a day's wages for every 20 miles.[8]

Prince Estabrook probably spent the next spring and summer working in Lexington on the Estabrook farm. He returned to military service from November 6, 1777, to April 1778. This time Estabrook was in Cambridge, Mass., guarding some of the thousands of British and Hessian prisoners held there after General John Burgoyne's defeat at Saratoga, N.Y.[9]

The Continental army was looking for long-term enlistments to shore up depleted ranks when Estabrook enlisted for six months in late July 1780. He was discharged April 7, 1781. Two months later, he signed up for another three years.

A military report in 1780 lists Estabrook's age as 39, his stature as 5 feet, 11 inches, his complexion as Negro, and his occupation as "a farmer." Six months later, another list shows his age as 40, his hair and eyes as black, and his height as 5 feet, 6 inches.[10]

Prince Estabrook's name on a Continental army payroll sheet

As a member of Colonel John Greaton's 3rd Massachusetts Regiment, in 1780, Estabrook was likely helping to build and maintain fortifications in New York's Hudson River Highlands area.

Estabrook likely wore his own clothing while he served in the Lexington and state militia, but he was issued a uniform when he joined the Continental army. From 1780 to 1782, the 3rd Massachusetts uniform was similar to that of other Continental army units from the commonwealth: breeches or overalls, a wool waistcoat or vest, and a long blue wool coat with white lapels. A slightly redesigned uniform issued in 1783 included a cocked wool felt hat. Pewter buttons on the older uniforms featured the raised abbreviations "Mass." and "Reg." across the bottom and the Roman numeral III across the middle. Later buttons from this regiment, found in the Highlands area, are also pewter, with the abbreviation "Mass." on top, the numeral three in the middle, and a drum with two crossed flags at the bottom.[11]

Estabrook probably carried a Committee of Public Safety musket, a copy of the standard British army "Brown Bess" or shortland-pattern musket. Under Provincial law, soldiers were also required to have a bayonet, cartridge pouch, and canteen.

Greaton's regiment was sent to Dobbs Ferry, N.Y., when General George Washington was threatening to mount a campaign to take New York City.[12] The troops acted mostly as scouts. They were a presence in the area and could check on British activities. From perches high above the Hudson River, colonial soldiers could count the masts on British ships in New York harbor with spyglasses, according to Alan Aimone, senior Special Collections librarian at the U.S. Military Academy Library at West Point. When Washington decided that focusing on Yorktown would be the best military option, Greaton's regiment remained in the Hudson Highlands, guarding prisoners and tending to the many wooden fortifications and shelters in the area.[13]

The rugged Highlands area is about 50 miles north of New York City and 90 miles south of Albany.[14] The roughly 10-mile square wedge between Peekskill and Newburgh is where the Hudson River breaks through the steep Appalachian mountain chain, offering a strategic defense against British warships. This area could be dangerous for Continental troops since there were pockets of Tories in the region, Aimone adds.

Great Britain acknowledged American independence on November 30, 1782, but the peace treaty wasn't concluded until September 3, 1783. Estabrook's name appears on a muster roll for the last time in October 1783. On November 3, 1783, the Massachusetts 3rd was disbanded at West Point.[15]

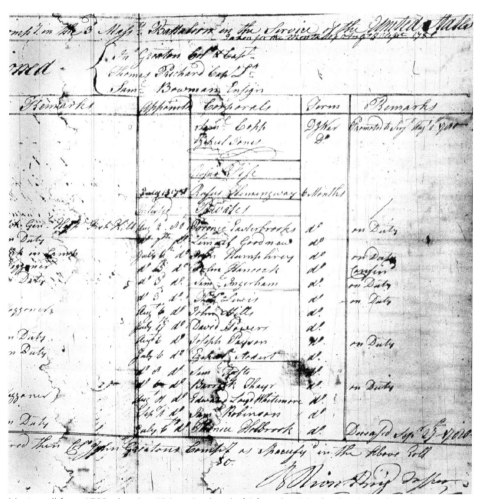

Muster roll from 1782, showing "Prince Estabrooks [sic] on duty" in the Continental army

After the war

Although there are only a few references to Prince Estabrook in official Lexington records, there are enough to determine that he returned to town after his discharge. He resumed his work with Benjamin and did odd jobs for residents around town.

Prince spent much of his time in the fields of Vine Brook Farm and possibly at the mill. Lexington Board of Selectmen's minutes also show he was paid 12 shillings for attending Mr. Isaac Stone "in his last illness & at his Death" in December 1786. Stone had been a prominent resident who, in 1761, presented Lexington with a bell weighing more than 450 pounds for the town's first "bell free."[1]

No documents have been found indicating when Prince Estabrook became a free man, but he is likely among the black patriots who gained independence for their war service. The 1790 census shows that the Lexington household Benjamin Estabrook headed included a non-white freeman (Prince) as a resident.[2] Prince's name also appears on several Lexington tax rolls in the 1790s, usually next to that of another former slave, Job Lock. On one tax roll, Estabrook and Lock's names were initially listed and then crossed out and entered at the end (most likely because of their race).[3] Prince was not taxed for property, which indicates that he moved from slave to employee of Benjamin Estabrook.

Stories of Prince Estabrook's role in the community include one that turned out to be pure fiction. It was described in a letter supposedly found nearly a century after the November 3, 1795, visit of George Washington to the Munroe Tavern.[4] (The nation's first president didn't sleep in Lexington, but he did eat there.)

On the 100th anniversary of the presidential visit, James P. Smith Munroe was asked to represent his great-grandfather, Lexington innkeeper William Munroe, at a celebration hosted by the Lexington Historical Society. In a speech James announced that he had recently discovered a letter written November 7, 1789, by William's daughter, Sarah, who had been among those welcoming Washington.

The letter, addressed to Miss Mary Mason of New York, described the president's visit and a splendid meal that included wine, fresh-brewed beer, flip,[5] roasted beef, a "showlder" of pork, squabs, puddings, and "pyes." The guests included selectmen and former soldiers "who had been in the fight," including Prince Estabrook. The letter noted that: "The Black man [Estabrook] . . . was being made acquainted, tho' stiffly, with Mr. Washington, and his servants." The letter was later labeled a fabrication, but the mention of Prince Estabrook suggests that he was well known in the community.

While no record of Prince Estabrook's marriage has been found, there is some reason to believe he once had a wife. Canavan refers to a time when Prince was courting a local woman and defended her ample size.[6]

Prince Estabrook's name appears on several Lexington tax rolls after the war. It was often listed separately at the end, along with the name of another former slave, Job Lock.

In a report to the Historical Society in 1902, Lexington historian and minister Reverend Carlton Staples wrote that Prince had been married but offered no evidence. Staples also said that children and young people were fond of Prince, who joined in their sports and games and told them stories.[7]

Despite dismal financial conditions rampant in the new country in the late 1700s, Benjamin Estabrook was relatively well off when he died in March 1803 at the age of 74. His personal effects and property were valued at more than $6,000, and he owned 330 acres, 200 of them in Townsend, adjacent to Ashby, Mass.[8] Benjamin's wife, Hannah, passed away at age 67, just two months before Benjamin died. Husband and wife were laid to rest next to each other in Lexington's Old Burying-Grounds. A joint epitaph reads:

> *Short was their separation, soon rejoined*
> *In the dark grave to native dust consigned*
> *There sleep till Death his human pray restore*
> *And earth & seas & skies shall be no more.*[9]

Benjamin and Hannah's three daughters—Hannah, Martha, and Millicent—married and moved away. Their six sons also scattered. Joseph IV went to Harvard College, was ordained as a pastor at Athol in 1787, and remained there until his death in 1830. Benjamin II married and lived for a time in Danvers, Mass. Samuel married after his first wife died. He lived in Brookline, Mass., and New Ipswich, N.H., then returned to Lexington before his death in 1814. Attai married Polly Pierce and remained in Lexington.[10]

Nathan, born in 1772, and Solomon, born in 1774, married women from New Ipswich, which borders Ashby. Nathan's wife, Sarah (Sally) Smith, was a Lexington school teacher from 1802 to 1804.[11] In 1804, Nathan was still one of Lexington's hog reeves.[12]

Solomon and Samuel were listed in the early 1800s as owners of the Estabrook Tavern in New Ipswich, a popular destination of [cattle] drovers.[13]

In 1805, the Estabrook family home in Lexington, including 38 acres of land, sold for $4,000. The deed allowed Attai and Nathan to continue part-time use of the mill and banned the new owner from setting up a competing mill in Vine Brook.[14]

Soon after the transaction, the house was dismantled and some timbers were used to build a nearby dwelling. A beam from the old parsonage is displayed in the lobby of Lexington's Cary Memorial Building, under the "Dawn of Liberty" painting, behind a wrought-iron railing.[15]

It was about 1805 when Prince Estabrook, then in his mid-sixties, left Lexington to live with Nathan in Ashby. At least a portion of Nathan's property stretched from Ashby into New Ipswich.[16] Attai moved into a house on what is now Lexington's Vine Street.[17] He held several town positions, including highway surveyor and district school committee member.[18]

Canavan gives no reason for his description of Attai as "shiftless, lazy, and slatternly,"[19] but signs of trouble began cropping up as early as 1807, when Attai and his wife, Polly, sold their pew in the meeting house.[20] Polly passed away November 6, 1826, and their son, Benjamin, died the same month from wounds received when a bullet "rebounded" or ricocheted.[21] Both Hudson's genealogical register and Lexington's vital records show only the month and year of young Benjamin's death, not the exact date. He was about 21 years old then. Attai sold off backland a little at a time until he died in 1836. His home was sold at public auction to settle the estate.[22]

Meanwhile, Nathan appears to have prospered in Ashby, where there was open land to farm and where he was near his wife's family, his brothers Solomon and Samuel, and other family members. Prince and Nathan also retained ties to Lexington. Canavan writes that the dying wish of one young Lexington girl was "to be buried in Ashby beside dear old Prince Estabrook."[23]

An eighteenth-century white clapboard farmhouse, once owned by a member of the Estabrook family, still stands in Ashby, along the road to New

Ipswich. According to legend, it was once Prince's home. Unfortunately, again, records that could have proved or disproved this have not been found.

Tradition, family histories, and accounts available in Lexington and in Ashby report that Ashby is where Prince Estabrook died in 1830, at the age of about 90.[24] No date of death or burial records, however, have been found there. The records might be missing because officials did not always record such information for African Americans, or they might be among the records that were lost or destroyed by fire.

Several Ashby residents recall that research confirming Estabrook's burial site was conducted by personnel from Fort Devens Army Base, in Ayer, Mass. Efforts to find that information after the Ayer base closed have been unsuccessful as yet.

A 1930 *Fitchburg Sentinel* newspaper article reports that Estabrook's name was found among those buried in the pauper's section of the Ashby First Parish Unitarian Universalist Church cemetery, where the graves of Nathan Estabrook and his wife, Sally, are located.[25] A headstone was later placed at Prince Estabrook's burial site by the U.S. War Department.

Estabrook's Ashby, Mass., burial site is marked.

In a ceremony dedicating the headstone on September 12, 1930, Fitchburg state representative Henry A. Estabrook hailed the slave and soldier as a "brave defender of American liberty." The late lawmaker was a descendant of the Estabrook family that once owned Prince.

The Massachusetts Society of the Sons of the American Revolution (SAR) bulletin, dated November 1930, states, in part: "The stone, a marble slab, was erected recently by the War Department after confirmation that, in the grave beneath, lay the body of Black Prince and that his record in the War Department was clear and enviable." The dedication was "upon the occasion of the Ashby Grande Fair" and was attended by the Laurence S. Ayer Post of the VFW, a drum and bugle corps, the Brigadier General James Reed Chapter, SAR, of Fitchburg, and official representatives of the Massachusetts Society SAR.[26]

In the late 1980s and early 1990s, services honoring Estabrook were held at the cemetery in Ashby each February, during Black History month. Each Memorial Day, Ashby residents place a flag at the burial site.

Estabrook's part in the April 19, 1775, clash is represented today in a diorama in Lexington's Visitor Center. His name is also inscribed on a war memorial opposite the Battle Green.

The 1949 dedication of a Revolutionary War monument. Prince Estabrook's name is engraved on the back of the marker.

A musty psalm book covered in worn brown leather is one of the few remaining objects with direct ties to Prince Estabrook. The psalm book's pages are yellow and faded. Some are frayed or torn at the edges. But this book is an exciting link to Estabrook. It provides new clues and brings him more into focus as a person. Estabrook himself found it in 1780 before leaving for his tour of duty. He later sold it to Buckman Tavern innkeeper Rufus Merriam, who would become Lexington's first postmaster.

This psalm book found and sold by Estabrook in 1780 is in the Lexington Historical Society's collection.

In 1894, Merriam's grand-daughter, Ellen Stetson, presented the book to the Lexington Historical Society. In 1995, the society's executive director George Comtois rediscovered it in the Hancock-Clarke House archives.[27] An inscription notes that Estabrook found the book on the roadside while traveling from Lexington to Watertown, Mass., to attend an ordination. Merriam paid 700 nearly worthless Continental dollars for the slim volume. The value of American currency had fallen so sharply that a pound of (Continental) paper money, worth 228 pence in January 1777, shrank in value to just three pence by January 1781. An iron kettle cost 1,200 Continental dollars on December 20, 1780.[28]

Watertown records from the 1700s indicate that Estabrook was heading to the ordination of minister Richard Eliot when the Lexington soldier spotted the psalm book. Eliot was a descendant of Minister John Eliot, known as the Apostle of the Indians for his work with Native Americans.[29]

Prejudice, controversy, and hope

Of the approximately 300,000 colonists who served in the Revolutionary War, at least 5,000 were African American, Native American, or biracial.[1] That number, however, may not reflect the full impact of these men's contributions. Many white soldiers served for short periods, sometimes only single campaigns, then returned to their farms or trades. White soldiers also signed up for multiyear terms, but black soldiers, in general, were more likely to serve longer. This was because they were seen as having less to lose and more to gain in the military than their white counterparts, according to author and historian Benjamin Quarles.[2]

Prejudice was woven into the fabric of colonial life in the northern colonies as well as in the South and on its plantations. Free and slave black colonists were normally segregated from white worshippers during meetinghouse services. Their vital records were entered haphazardly, if at all. They were usually buried in unmarked corners of cemeteries, and subsequent burial-site markers were often placed in approximate locations. Most slaves were discouraged from learning to read and write. Married slaves were often forced to live apart from their spouses and families, and their children could be sold.[3]

Military policy toward Revolutionary War soldiers of color was marked by indecision, confusion, and inconsistency. In New England, when the Revolutionary War began, both free and enslaved African Americans were initially accepted for military service. However, as early as April 19, 1775, there were fears, and even some panic, about a possible slave uprising while militia companies were on duty outside their own towns.[4]

A committee weighing the use of black soldiers in the Continental army decided in May 1775 that only freemen should be admitted to the military. On

June 6, a resolution was sent to Congress recommending "that no slave be admitted into the army, upon any consideration whatsoever." By October 8, 1775, Continental army generals agreed to reject both slaves and free Negroes.[5]

This and subsequent state militia bans, however, were widely ignored, and many positive reports about the service of African-American soldiers were recorded. Black patriot Salem Poor of Andover, Mass., was commended by his superiors for the courage and skill he displayed in the Battle of Bunker Hill. In June 1775, in his *Notes to His Sketch of Bunker-Hill Battle*, Samuel Swett writes, "Many northern blacks were excellent soldiers, but southern troops would not brook an equity with whites."[6]

In the fall of 1775, General John Thomas, commander of a Roxbury, Mass., brigade, wrote, "We have some Negroes; but I look on them, in General, Equally Serviceable with other men, for Fatigue & in action; many of them have proved themselves brave."[7]

Other white leaders and troops, however, didn't hide their distaste for serving with soldiers of color. In July of 1776, Captain Persifor Frazer of the 4th Pennsylvania battalion wrote to his wife, noting that the Yankee regiments were composed, in part, of "the strangest mixture of Negroes, Indians, and white, with old men and mere children, which together with a nasty lousy appearance, make a most shocking spectacle."[8]

In a July 1777 letter home, General Philip Schuyler complained that the soldiers assigned to him were mostly boys, old men, or black men. "The last disgrace our arms. Is it consistent with the Sons of Freedom to trust their all to be defended by slaves?" he wrote.[9]

One can only imagine the atmosphere of tension that must have existed in camps where white soldiers with these views lived and fought side by side with soldiers of color.

Meanwhile, in November 1775, Virginia's royal governor John Murray, earl of Dunmore, issued a proclamation offering slaves liberty and protection if they fought for the crown. Murray's initiative was largely unsuccessful for many

A copy of Lord Dunmore's proclamation

reasons, including the anger it raised among loyalist southern slave owners and British leaders who were horrified to think of slaves being urged to flee their masters and carry weapons. The policy, however, paved the way for later successful attempts by the British to convince slaves that their best shot for freedom was fighting against the upstart colonials. By the war's end, thousands of slaves had accepted the offer. When the British were defeated, more than 1,000 slaves who had cast their lot with the Redcoats were evacuated. Some went to the west coast of Africa, some to central Europe, and the majority to the British Caribbean Islands or Canada.[10]

Realizing that the opportunity to trade military service for freedom touched the deepest hopes and dreams of slaves, Continental army leaders struggled with their own enlistment policies. By January 1776, General George Washington was again permitting enlistment of "Free negroes who have served faithfully in the Army, no others."[11] Adding even more confusion, militia organizations in individual states were adopting their own new enlistment regulations. On April 12, 1776, the New Hampshire Committee of Safety decreed that all males above 21 must sign a declaration pledging themselves to oppose British hostilities with arms. "Lunatics, idiots, and Negroes" were the exceptions.[12]

In early 1776, the Massachusetts Militia Act banned "Negroes, Indians, and mulattos" from enlisting. Later that year, the state's lawmakers closed a potential loophole by tacking wording onto a law intended to raise funds and manpower for the war effort. It stated that white soldiers could not "procure any person to [take up arms] in their room [place]." By the summer of 1776, other New England states banned enlistment of black soldiers.[13]

These policies of exclusion were partly rooted in hopes that the war would end quickly. Those hopes had dimmed by the summer of 1777, when yet another Continental army policy was in the works. It acknowledged the need to boost manpower by loosening racial restrictions. By 1777, Massachusetts again began allowing soldiers of color to serve, passing a law that exempted "only Quakers" from military service. The following year African Americans were officially included among those permitted to enlist.[14]

While military leaders sparred over this issue, black soldiers continued to unofficially contribute on land and sea, in combat, as messengers, and by carrying out routine military duties. In 1778, Rhode Island assembled a 125-man black regiment with white officers, a unit that served with great distinction in several battles.[15]

It was the desperate need for more troops that helped break down most remaining racial barriers by 1779. In March, Alexander Hamilton urged Congress to recruit more African-American soldiers. "If we do not make use of them in this way, the enemy probably will," he said pragmatically.[16]

In 1780, French General Rochambeau's aide-de-camp, Baron Ludwig von Closen, described the good spirits of black troops at White Plains, N.Y., in his journal. "A quarter of them [American soldiers] were Negroes, merry, confident, and sturdy," he wrote.[17]

By 1781, more states were promising freedom to slaves who would serve in the army for three years or until discharged. Before the war ended, it became common to promise freedom to slaves who would enlist.[18] Records show three black patriots from Bedford, Mass., gained their freedom this way.[19]

According to Quarles, the black Revolutionary soldier's "major loyalty was not to a place nor a people, but to a principle . . . . Whoever invoked the image of liberty, be he American or British, could count on a ready response from the blacks."[20]

The typical African-American Revolutionary War soldier was a private, according to Quarles. More often than other soldiers, the black soldier "tended to lack identity" and "sometimes was carried on the rolls as A Negro Man or Negro by Name or Negro, Name unknown," he says.[21]

Quarles suggests, however, that this type of treatment did not appear to significantly affect the willingness or ability of black men to serve. Despite its discomforts and dangers, military service, the author concludes, was often a step forward for most black soldiers.[22] It is also clear that the effort of black soldiers contributed to the ultimate American victory.

Many African Americans had hoped that the Declaration of Independence would spell out their freedom in no uncertain terms. In fact, Thomas Jefferson had included a passage condemning the slave trade in a draft of the Declaration of Independence written in December 1775. By July 4, 1776, however, that passage had been removed.[23] In 1777, Vermont became the first state to prohibit slavery by constitutional provision.[24]

Slavery officially ended in Massachusetts in 1780 with the approval of a Massachusetts Declaration of Rights that stated, in part, "All men are born free and equal."[25] In practice, however, to legally obtain his or her freedom, a slave would have to go to court, citing the law.[26] In a ruling in 1783, the same year the peace treaty with Great Britain was finally signed, Massachusetts Supreme Court chief justice William Cushing confirmed that slavery could no longer exist in the commonwealth.[27]

The United States that emerged from the Revolution had been shaped on a foundation of individual freedom and equality. In the North, this yearning for political liberty intertwined with efforts to achieve social justice, and led, by the early 1800s, to policies for gradual abolition of slavery in all northern states.[28]

Weary soldiers trudge uphill.

It was a different story in the South, where much of the economy and culture was tied to slave labor. Abolition threatened the plantations and the southern way of life. Fundamental clashes over slavery and property rights soon started unraveling the new nation, hardening into a distinction between "slave" and "free" states. It would take a painful civil war and nearly a century for the two sides to reconcile.[29]

While life for African Americans in the North may not have improved as much as black patriots had hoped it would after the Revolutionary War, Native Americans lost both land and political voice. Most members of Indian tribes either stayed out of the military or fought for the British, but hundreds joined the colonists, risking their lives and pinning their hopes on the Revolution's lofty ideals.[30]

In Massachusetts, perhaps the most well-known Native American patriots hailed from Stockbridge. About 30 warriors signed up for the colonial militia months before the Revolutionary War began. Seventeen of the "Stockbridges" enlisted in the provincial Army, joining Washington's troops in Cambridge in the spring of 1775. As the war continued, their ranks grew, and these soldiers were cited for their bravery, earning a reputation for "zealous service."[31]

Tragedy struck for them in the summer of 1778, near White Plains, N.Y. The Stockbridge unit was ambushed, and a chief and his son were among 17 Native Americans confirmed dead. More died later from illnesses or injuries suffered in the campaign.

In return for their loyalty and sacrifices, many members of the once vibrant Stockbridge Native American community, including widows with young children, had to sell their property to pay debts. Gradually, the remaining Native Americans from several tribes were forced to leave the place where they had thrived before the land-hungry colonials arrived.[32]

The story of the Stockbridge American Indian community reflects experiences of Native Americans in other parts of the United States. To learn more about this chapter in America's history, read Colin G. Calloway's *The American Revolution in Indian Country.*

Progress "deadly slow"

Lexington Minute Man and reenactor Charles Price still finds it hard to understand why Prince Estabrook remains relatively unknown. Price suspects the primary reasons Estabrook was initially ignored are obvious: "He was black. He was a slave. And he couldn't read or write. Basically, no one was interested in what he thought or felt."[1]

While Prince may have been relatively well treated by the Estabrook family, the fact remains that, until slavery was abolished in Massachusetts, slaves were legally considered as property and were bought and sold.[2] Often nameless, they can be found casually listed in wills and property inventories next to tallies of horses, oxen, and bushels of corn.[3]

1742 inventory of John Esterbrooks' [sic] estate

Price, however, thinks it is important for Americans to remember that black and white soldiers served and fought side by side on April 19, 1775, and during most of the Revolutionary War. It would not happen again for nearly two centuries.

Although the Emancipation Proclamation officially ended slavery in all states by 1863, the lack of respect accorded black troops hadn't changed significantly by the time Price joined the army during the Korean War.

"While President Harry Truman began to desegregate the military in the late 1940s," Price says, "my unit in the Korean War was 100 percent segregated, and discrimination was alive and well while I was a soldier." As a field artillery platoon sergeant, the prejudice Price experienced was overt, personal, and degrading. For example, "at the train station near Fort Sill army base in Oklahoma, even in uniform, the conductor told you to move to the back of the train if you weren't white, and he didn't tell you pleasantly either," Price says.[4]

Out of uniform, he adds, the prejudice was even more pervasive. After the Korean War ended, he remembers trying to find lodging in a New Mexico motel along Route 66. "The response [at the motel desk] was: 'We don't serve colored people.' I felt like saying: When I got called up [to the Army], no one asked about my color. I was so tired that night, though; I just kept quiet and moved on," he says.

Ironically, Price's unit, the 272nd Field Artillery Battalion, is a descendant of the 372nd Infantry, which earned the French Croix de Guerre for distinguished service during WWI. "Those [WWI] troops were honored by the French government because this segregated unit served with French forces. They weren't allowed to fight with 'the Americans,' " Price explains.[5]

For Price, growing up black in the 1940s meant living in a world where most of the people he saw doing exciting things, people in roles of leadership, were white. There was an important exception—his father, who was a Boston police officer and a hero to Price and his friends.

"I remember movies that showed white cowboys—*of course*—fighting Indians, savages who *always* did terrible bloody things to the settlers. Years pass, and then you find out that there actually *were* black cowboys, and you learn that the Indians had been on these lands for thousands of years before the white men came. They were fighting to protect their homelands from invasion by 'foreigners.' If I were fighting for my home, I would fight ferociously, too," Price says. "More revelations came with the book and TV series *Roots*, which presented the early American saga of slavery with an intensity many white Americans had been comfortably unaware of," according to Price.

Meanwhile, with the encouragement of his parents, Price was planning an ambitious future. "No one from my family had ever gone to college, but I felt that if I got the chance to go, I would work hard to succeed," he says. When his National Guard unit was called to active duty during the Korean War, Price was already studying engineering at Northeastern University in Boston, where he returned after the war.

"My mother didn't live to see it happen, but my father encouraged me all along the way," Price says. His dad was among those watching when Price received a graduate degree in electrical engineering from Northeastern in 1960.

Price in the Army, 1952

Price as reenactor today

"Since Martin Luther King took to the streets with his protest marches, there has been some progress toward real equality. Black faces are now seen more often in all facets of our life, including movies, TV, and major league sports. However, in the business world, gains have been much slower," Price says.

Price credits the fact that he can freely travel in parts of the South, where he was unwelcome as a graduate student, in large measure to "Rosa Parks, a very brave lady, and to two men who were giants on the American scene, Supreme Court Justice Thurgood Marshall and the Reverend Dr. Martin Luther King Jr.

"Rosa Parks stared into the face of ugly, hostile segregation and refused to give up her seat and go to the back of the bus. Her actions, risking personal injury, provided the spark that led to the protest marches," Price says.

"Long before becoming a Supreme Court justice, Thurgood Marshall led a legal team that struggled relentlessly to overturn laws designed to keep blacks as second-class citizens (*Brown vs. the Board of Education*)," Price adds.

"And Martin Luther King, with his nonviolent demonstrations and brilliant orations seeking justice for all, brought so much public pressure to bear that federal laws had to change . . . . These people are my heroes. They learned how to work within the system and caused the system to change," according to Price.

"Still, we've got a long way to go, and sometimes, it seems like our progress is deadly slow," he says.[6] Price believes that letting more people know about Prince Estabrook might help speed up the process.

"I think people should know there was a black man who took part in that first battle of the Revolution, someone who thought enough of his country and his community to go out and risk his life, long before freedom for slaves was established in this country. For people whose minds are open, it might affect the way they look at things in their own lives today," he says.

"It wasn't a grand design for me to portray Prince Estabrook, because I didn't even know he existed when I joined the Lexington Minute Men," Price says. "Still, today I feel extra proud when I walk by the Minute Man statue on Lexington Green. I can look up and say, I was a commander of the Lexington militia, too. I stood in those shoes, and I've helped pass on the torch," he adds.

Several years ago when he learned where Prince Estabrook was buried, Price, with his wife, Imelda, and Lexington Minute Man John Chancholo and his wife, Cindy, visited the burial site in Ashby. "I was surprised at how much I felt for this black man who fought for freedom more than 200 years ago," Price says. "Walking toward the marker was quite emotional. Here was a man whose part I've been portraying and, when I saw his grave, I felt a bond, a strange sort of empathy. We put a flag at his burial site, stood back and gave him a salute," Price says. "I remember thinking of the scene in *Roots* when author Alex Haley discovers the grave of his ancestor and exclaims, 'You old African, at last I've found you.' "[7]

Charles Price in Lexington Minute Men dress uniform at the Minute Man Statue

Appendix A
More unsung heroes

My search for material on Prince Estabrook brought unexpected dividends—descriptions, facts, and anecdotes that help bring to life the stories of dozens of other patriots of color who served from communities west and north of Boston. The efforts of some of these men, including Peter Salem, Salem Poor, and Barzillai Lew, received a measure of recognition. Most have been forgotten. The following glimpses into their lives reflect the efforts of thousands of others who embraced the cause of liberty and fought for America's freedom. Before the War for Independence ended, black patriots were serving throughout the new nation, and lawmakers in most states had endorsed the enlistment of these men, both free and slave.

Andover—Salem Poor honored for bravery at Bunker Hill

Salem Poor, a freeman from Andover, Mass., left a wife and family to enlist in Colonel Frye's regiment, Captain Benjamin Ames's company, soon after the war began. Poor is best known for the courage he showed during the Battle of Bunker Hill in June of 1775. Although the colonists were driven back, Poor was cited for his bravery in action.

A petition asking that he be recognized was signed December 5, 1775, by 14 officers in the field during the battle. They described Poor as a "brave and gallant soldier," who in "the late battle at Charlestown, behaved like an experienced officer, as well as an excellent soldier." They went on to say that it would be "tedious" to go into more detail about his

This U. S. postal stamp honoring Salem Poor was issued on March 25, 1975.

Pomp Lovejoy's burial site

heroic conduct, adding, "We only beg leave to say, in the person of this said negro centers a brave and gallant soldier."[1] There is no record of an official commendation, but a stamp honoring Poor was issued in 1975. Poor also served during the Siege of Boston, in Valley Forge, Pa., and in White Plains, N.Y. He was discharged March 1, 1780.[2]

Other black patriots from Andover included: Caesar Russell,[3] Prince Johnnot,[4] Cato Foster,[5] Cato Freeman (or Freman),[6] and Pompey (or Pomp) Lovejoy.[7] Lovejoy, a freed slave who marched in the April 19, 1775, alarm, built a cabin on the shore of an Andover pond that was later named Pomps Pond in his honor. Lovejoy and his wife, Rose, settled there, farmed nearby land, and Pomp fished and swam in the pond. Local accounts say Lovejoy would celebrate election day by dispensing his homemade rootbeer to townspeople. He was 102 when he died in 1826.[8]

One Andover history notes that Lovejoy gained his freedom at age 38 and that he was "much respected as a sensible, amiable and upright man." Lovejoy is buried in Andover's South Church Cemetery. His gravestone reads, "Born in Boston a slave, died in Andover a free man. Feb. 23, 1826."[9]

The record of Cato Freeman notes that he was among those who reported "unfit for duty" in early January 1781. A subsequent notice shows his bounty was officially stipulated as "freedom in three years."[10] Born a slave, Freeman lived with the families of Samuel Phillips and his son, Judge Phillips, who introduced Freeman to many of their distinguished visitors. A letter Freeman wrote May 24, 1789, on leaving the family's service, expresses gratitude for kindness, care, and checks. The letter is preserved in the North Andover Historical Society archives. Freeman died in 1853 at age 85.[11]

In a January 1781 military list, Foster is described as an Andover resident, 22 years old, 5 feet 5 inches tall, with black hair and complexion. He was a drummer in several companies, and his name is on a "list of men entitled to 200 acres of land for his service."[12]

Arlington—Lamson leads Old Men of Menotomy

In the town of Menotomy (now Arlington, Mass.), David Lamson, a biracial or part Native American, led a band of unlikely Revolutionary War heroes on the afternoon of April 19, 1775.[1]

With young, able-bodied men off to Concord and Lexington, a group of about 12 elderly men learned that a British supply convoy was headed to town on its way to Lexington with supplies and ammunition. The men, members of the town's alarm (or emergency) company, became famous that day as the Old Men of Menotomy. It is likely they chose Lamson as their leader because of his experience in the French and Indian Wars. His plan was simple: wait in ambush behind a stone wall near the meeting house, then attack.[2]

Although surprised by the makeshift force, the British refused to stop their wagons. Lamson and the elderly men pulled out their muskets and opened fire, killing two Redcoats and several horses. The supply-train driver and several British guards reportedly ran toward nearby Spy Pond, tossing their guns in the water so the weapons wouldn't fall into rebel hands.[3]

Lamson and his crew brought the wagons they had seized to a nearby area where the town train station would later be built. Meanwhile, an elderly Menotomy woman, Mother Batherick, saw soldiers running toward her from Spy Pond near her home. Batherick was reportedly digging dandelions when the British soldiers asked for her protection and surrendered. Batherick brought them to Ephraim Frost's house on Pleasant Street. According to one story, Batherick told them, "If you ever live to get back to England, you tell the king that an old woman took six British grenadiers prisoner."[4]

Lamson served at Dorchester Heights in 1776 and earned 20 shillings and 6 pence supplying General Washington's army with beef. The following year he was a member of Colonel Josiah Whitney's regiment in Rhode Island.[5]

Paul Hogman, past captain of the modern-day Menotomy Minute Men, says that if the British wagons had reached Percy's troops, the ammunition and supplies they carried might have influenced the outcome of the later battle near the Jason Russell House, where the Regulars suffered serious losses.

The Old Men of Menotomy's bravery is commemorated today with a stone marker outside the First Parish Church, on Massachusetts Avenue in Arlington Center. The area where the captured wagons once stood has been renamed David Lamson Way. Menotomy Minute Men annually reenact the battle at the Jason Russell House, along with the exploits of Lamson, the Old Men, and Mother Batherick.[6]

Black patriots Cuff Whittemore [7] and Cato Wood,[8] members of Captain Benjamin Locke's Menotomy company, were among the African Americans in action on April 19, 1775. Their unit was engaged in the fierce battle near the Jason Russell House as the British retreated.

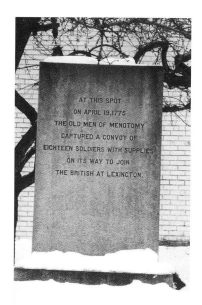

Men of Menotomy memorial

A later account of the Battle of Bunker Hill by Samuel Swett noted that Whittemore "fought to the last" and received a ball through his hat. Miraculously escaping injury, Whittemore reportedly picked up a British officer's sword lying loose on the field, which he later sold.[9]

Whittemore, the slave of Menotomy teacher William Whittemore, again displayed his courage and quick thinking as a Continental army private. Captured by the British at the time of Burgoyne's surrender, he managed to escape, taking two horses with him. After dodging a shower of enemy bullets while fording a stream with the horses, Whittemore received a warm welcome back at the Continental lines, according to reports.[10] His mark (*X*) is on a pension application dated April 1, 1818. The pension was granted.[11]

Bedford—Black patriots honored in African Reservation

A stone in the northeast corner of the Old Burying Ground, on Springs Road in Bedford, Mass., marks the burial site of Caesar Jones, Cambridge Moore, and Caesar Prescott. These men were laid to rest with at least a dozen other persons in a common burial area known as the "African Reservation."[1]

A marker in Bedford's African Reservation pays tribute to three black patriots.

Jones,[2] Moore,[3] and Prescott[4] all served with distinction in the Continental army for the greater part of the Revolutionary War, each with a different regiment. Family traditions suggest that Caesar Jones and Cambridge Moore joined their masters in Concord on April 19, 1775,[5] but no proof has been found. In a descriptive list from December 1780, Prescott is listed as age 40, 5 feet 8 inches tall, with black complexion and eyes. All three gained freedom for their service.[6]

Another former slave, Peter Freeman,[7] earned his independence, then worked for the Stearns family in Bedford until enlisting. He died of consumption on May 7, 1807, at the age of 57.[8] He was initially buried in the African Reservation, but his remains were later moved to Shawsheen Cemetery in Bedford, near the Stearns family plot.[9]

Information about these black Revolutionary soldiers was compiled in 1976 and is now a part of the Bedford Free Public Library's Bedford Collection.[10]

Cambridge—Bordman and Stedman in action on April 19

At least two black patriots from Cambridge, Mass., Cato Bordman[1] and Cato Stedman,[2] were in action on April 19, 1775. Both served one day in Captain Samuel Thatcher's militia. Stedman's name is also on a May 27, 1777, list of men raised for the Continental army. He was assigned to Captain Cleaton's (Slayton's) company. Bordman was among the troops who signed up in 1776 as reinforcements for the Northern Army and served in the Fort Ticonderoga area.

Another Cambridge black man, Neptune Frost,[3] volunteered for service in the fall of 1776. He was dispatched to Horse Neck, N.Y., and discharged 13 months later. He served as a drummer in two different companies and guarded prisoners in Cambridge and Charlestown from January to April 1778. When Frost enlisted in the Continental army on August 7, 1780, he was described as a laborer, 28 years old, 5 feet 3 inches tall, with black complexion and hair. Frost signed up for a three-year Continental army term in December of 1781. Stedman and Frost were laid to rest in Cambridge's Old Burying Ground.

Chelmsford, Dracut—Lew is drummer, fifer, frontline soldier

Barzillai Lew was born in Groton, Mass., in 1743. He lived in Chelmsford, Mass., from 1772 to 1776, then moved to Dracut, Mass.[1] Lew served for Chelmsford in the Revolutionary War. Military records describe him as 6 feet tall and 30 years of age.[2] In 1778, he bought the first of three parcels of land in a section of Dracut that later became part of Lowell, Mass.[3] Lew died in Dracut in 1822 and is buried in an unmarked grave in the long-abandoned Clay Pit Cemetery, in what is also now Lowell.[4]

A free man and a cooper, or barrelmaker, by trade, Lew fought with the King's forces in the French and Indian Wars. About 1767, he purchased Dinah Bowman's freedom for $400 and married her. A talented musician, Lew was a fifer and a drummer as well as a frontline soldier during the Revolutionary War.[5]

His military leader at Fort Ticonderoga, Captain Joseph Bradley Varnum of Dracut, wrote on November 1, 1777, that Lew (also called "Zeal") was selected as "a fifer and fiddler for the grand appearance the day that Burgoyne's Famous Army [was] brought in. A Wonderful Show."[6] Lew had earlier served at Bunker Hill.

Family members believe that this is a portrait of Barzillai Lew. It hangs in the State Department building.

After the war, Lew, his wife, Dinah, and their large family formed a musical group that performed across New England.[7] One history of Dracut reports that the musicians were in such demand in Boston that some Lew family members lived there during the winter. The account says Barzillai Jr. was tall, handsome, dignified, remarkably intelligent, and refined. It adds, "Had it not been for the social degradation to which the race he belonged to had been reduced, he would have been elected to the first offices in his town, if not the state."[8] Some of Lew's descendants were later involved in the underground railroad, a network of abolitionists who found places to shelter runaway slaves on their flight to Canada.

A portrait called "The Flutist," which hangs in the Walter Thurston Gentlemen's Room of the State Department building in Washington, D.C., is believed by the Lew family to be the likeness of Barzillai. His powder horn is in the permanent collection at the DuSable Museum of African-American History in Chicago. It was placed there by Gerard Lew, one of the museum's founders and a descendant of Barzillai.[9]

Over the years, Lew's descendants distinguished themselves in many fields, including music and sports. The musicians included Edith Lew White, a soprano who performed in the Boston area in the late 1800s, and Carl Lew White, who was in a trio with entertainer Paul Robeson in the 1920s and was the first African American man known to have sung in a Boston cafe in the early 1900s.[10]

Harry Bucky Lew, a violinist, was also the nation's first black professional basketball player, according to his daughter, Phyllis Lew. Harry played basketball in Lowell and organized a team of professionals that traveled in New England.[11] Phyllis Lew hopes her father's achievements will be recognized in the Basketball Hall of Fame and that Barzillai Lew's burial site in Lowell will someday be marked.[12]

Concord—Servants enlist to help fill town quota

Black patriots from Concord, Mass., included Philip Barrett, Brister Freeman, Caesar Minot, and Casey Whitney. Barrett enlisted in July 1775, and signed up for six months' service in October 1780 to help satisfy a town quota. On July 14, 1780, Barrett was listed as 19 years old, 5 feet 9 inches tall, with Negro complexion. He was discharged at West Point in January 1781.[1]

Caesar Minot, a private in Captain Abijah Wyman's company, is among the men on a muster roll in Cambridge dated October 3, 1775. His record includes a February 9, 1776, document signed by Wyman. It certifies that Minot failed to get a bounty coat for three months' service in 1775. Minot is also on a list of men raised, in 1779, to serve a three-year term in the Continental army.[2]

According to D. Michael Ryan, Concord Minute Men historian, records of the Concord militia companies in 1775 suggest that Philip Barrett was present during at least one militia gathering. At the time, however, Philip was only 14 years old and may have been listed because he was accompanying his master.[3]

Brister (Cuming) Freeman was the slave of Concord Town Meeting moderator and physician Colonel John Cuming. Caesar Minot's owner was militia Captain George Minot, and Casey's master was Samuel Whitney. Casey (or Case) Whitney enlisted in the Army for a three-year term, serving for the town of Lancaster.[4]

Whitney's troubles with his master's family were described by Henry David Thoreau in his 1858 journal. According to Thoreau, Whitney may have been stolen from Africa when he was 20, leaving a wife and child. Thoreau also wrote that once, when [Casey] was chopping wood, his master's son pelted him with snowballs and [Casey] threw his ax at the son. Facing jail, Casey fled. He "hid himself in the river up to his neck till nightfall," then left to enlist. Casey "used to say he went home to Africa in the night and came back again in the morning," the journal entry continues.[5] Whitney was set free for his military service and returned to Concord after the war, Ryan says.

Freeman served under Colonel John Buttrick at Saratoga in 1777. He enlisted again July 20, 1779. That year, on a Continental army list, Freeman is described as 31 years old, 5 feet 7 inches tall, with Negro complexion.[6] He earned his freedom and was discharged April 20, 1780. Freeman returned to Concord after the war, married, and settled there.[7]

In *The Black Presence in the Revolutionary Era*, historian and author Sydney Kaplan writes that Freeman's war efforts didn't prevent harrassment. One story tells of a white neighbor who once tricked Freeman into an encounter with an angry bull and laughed as Freeman fought for his life. Later, Kaplan continued, Freeman was known as "a very passionate man" who would not suffer "boys who loved to insult and plague him."[8]

Framingham—Peter Salem responds to the alarm

Reenactor Bruce Harris portrays Peter Salem in Minute Man National Historical Park.

Peter Salem, a former slave from Framingham, Mass., was a private in Captain Simon Edgell's company of Minute Men, a unit that responded on April 19, 1775.[1]

Some claim that Salem is the African-American soldier depicted in Trumbull's painting of Bunker Hill and that he killed British Major John Pitcairn in the Battle of Bunker Hill, but many have questioned the accuracy of those accounts.[2] After the war, Salem returned to Framingham. He later settled in Leicester, Mass., where he earned a living weaving cane seats for chairs. A street in the Leicester area where he once lived is named Peter Salem Road.[3]

When Salem grew old and could not support himself, Leicester officials sent him back to Framingham. His former owners and Framingham officials made sure Salem would be supported for the rest of his life, according to Stephen Herring, town historian. Salem was buried in the paupers' section of Framingham's Old Burying Ground. His name and the major battles in which he participated are engraved on a marker near his burial site.[4] Today, Salem's story, including his participation in the Bloody Angle fight on April 19, 1775, is recounted in programs at Minute Man National Historical Park. The park's curator, Teresa Wallace, has written a thought-provoking paper on Salem's life.

Lexington—Burdoo, Blackman among the town's black patriots

In 1775, Lexington had 700 residents. By 1790, the population had jumped to 941.[1] About 215 men served for the town at some time during the Revolutionary War. At least nine, or about one in every 24, were African American. They included Estabrook, Eli and Silas Burdoo, Pompey Blackman, Samuel Crafts, Pompey Fisk, Cato Tudor, John Tingle, and Jupiter Tree.[2] Some may have been nonresidents recruited to fill the town's military quota, but most had direct ties to Lexington.

Eli Burdoo was a private in Captain Parker's Lexington company. He is listed as serving on April 19, 1775, and at Cambridge during the Battle of Bunker Hill, in May and in June 1775.[3] Eli had been baptized in Lexington on July 20, 1755.[4] His cousin, Silas Burdoo, was a private in Captain John Wood's 5th regiment.[5]

The Burdoo (also spelled Burdeau) family lived on Bedford Road (now Bedford Street) nearly opposite the old Simonds Tavern.[6] Eli's name and the names of other family members often show up in town records and legal documents as persons to whom payment was given or owed for services. Both Eli and Silas later moved out of Lexington. Some members of the Burdoo family settled outside of Jaffrey, N.H. Others moved to Vermont.[7]

Although the Lexington author and historian Charles Hudson referred to the Burdoo family as "colored," he included their name in the main alphabetical listing of his town genealogical records, rather than under the separate "Negro" heading, perhaps because they were free. Following the Burdoo name, in the 1868 edition of his *History of Lexington*, Hudson noted: "As God has made of one blood all nations of men, there is no reason why we should not notice a very respectable colored family which resided many years in town and discharged all the duties of citizens."[8]

Blackman arrived in Lexington in 1773. A notice to selectmen on April 4, 1773, states that John Simonds "has taken in One Pompey Blackman, a Negro." Blackman's last residence was listed as Woburn, "where his late master was Nathan Wyman." Blackman first served in Colonel Laommi Baldwin's Woburn regiment and fought on April 19 in Lincoln and Arlington. He was stationed in Roxbury during the Siege of Boston in 1776 and was in Fort Ticonderoga with Prince Estabrook in 1777.[9]

On April 2, 1777, Blackman signed his mark (*X*) on a power of attorney agreement. It gave his "trusty friend" Amos Fortune (who moved from Woburn, Mass., to Jaffrey) the authority to act in Blackman's interests when money was due him while Blackman was in the service.[10]

The former Burdoo family home, shown in 1924, still stands in Lexington, Mass.

RETREAT OF THE BRITISH FROM LEXINGTON.

Pompey Blackman was among the militiamen who confronted the retreating Redcoats. This print was in the October 30, 1858, issue of Ballou's *Pictorial Drawing Room Companion*.

In 1778, Lexington Captain Edmund Munroe wrote to his wife from Valley Forge, Pa., that Blackman was ailing but on the mend.[11] Blackman was baptized in 1782 in Lexington and died there a year later.[12]

Jupiter Tree and Samuel Crafts were also members of Munroe's company. Tree's service, from 1777 to 1780, included duty in Providence, R.I. "A Negro, Jupiter," is among the Lexington deaths recorded in 1781. It may refer to Jupiter Tree, but the death record does not list a surname.[13]

Crafts served at Fishkill, N.Y., and was marked in attendance on a 1781 muster roll from West Point.[14] Pompey Fisk was on military duty from May of 1775 to early 1776.[15] No records found thus far show if these soldiers were slaves or freemen prior to the war, but the Fisk family did have at least one slave in 1775.

Cato Tudor was 21 years old and 5 feet 4 inches tall in 1780, when he joined a unit raised to reinforce the Continental army. His six months of service began in June.[16] Tudor may have been a Boston resident hired to meet Lexington's quota. John Tingle was on duty in Cambridge during the Battle of Bunker Hill and from late 1776 until February 1777. He earned an allowance for travel from Boston to Bennington, Vt., but his record ends abruptly with desertion on July 26, 1778.[17]

Lincoln—Scippio Brister's burial site marked

Sippeo, or Scippio, Brister,[1] the slave of John Hoar, was one of four black patriots from Lincoln. Also listed as Brister, or Bristol, Hoar was 21 when he participated in the Saratoga campaign in 1777. According to John C. MacLean, author and past president of the Lincoln Historical Society, Brister died November 1, 1820. He is buried in the Precinct Burial Ground section of Lincoln's Lexington Road Cemetery, just below a ridge where the common grave of five British soldiers is marked.

Brister's burial site in Lincoln is near the common graves of five British soldiers.

Brister returned to live with his former master John Hoar's family after the war. The early eighteenth-century Hoar farmhouse still stands on the north side of Route 2, nearly opposite Lexington Road.[2]

Peter Sharon,[3] Peter Bowes,[4] and Jack Farrar[5] were three other African Americans serving from Lincoln. Sharon was 18 when he signed up for three years in early 1781. He died in Lincoln during the winter of 1792–93. Bowes, a private from 1777 until the war's end, was paying a Lincoln poll tax by 1783. After the war, the heirs of Amos Brooks deeded Bowes a one-acre woodland near Flint's Pond. Farrar, originally a slave in the George Farrar family, was variously listed as John Farrar, Jack Hatch, and Jack Freeman. His Continental army service included a winter at Valley Forge. He died in 1787.[6]

Littleton—Black patriot's name on war monument

In Littleton, Mass., the name of Scipio,[1] an African American, is among those engraved on a Revolutionary War monument in that town's Liberty Square. Scipio's surname was Chase and his first name was spelled at least three different ways. He was married in 1766 and died in 1788, at the age of 52.[2]

Medford—"A life of slavery is far worse than Nonexistence."

Six African Americans named Prince Hall are listed as Revolutionary War soldiers, three with ties to Medford, Mass. It is likely that one of those is the self-educated freed slave who founded the first lodge of black freemasons.[1] Hall was a strong advocate for equal rights for African Americans and for the abolition of slavery. In January of 1777, he was among the black citizens who signed a petition to the General Court demanding that slavery be abolished.

The petition, while ultimately unsuccessful, states that the very reason motivating America's break with England "pleads stronger than a thousand arguments in favor of your humble petitioners." It also notes that "a life of slavery is far worse than Nonexistence."[2] Primus Freeman from Medford, son of the lodge's founder, also served in the Revolutionary War.[3]

Reading and Stoneham—Five black patriots pick surname Freeman

When they gained their freedom, some former slaves proudly chose first names or surnames that reflected their new status, such as Liberty, Free, or Freeman.[1] In Massachusetts alone, more than 200 soldiers with the surname Freeman served in the Revolutionary War, at least a dozen of them with the first name Cato.[2]

Jonas,[3] Doss,[4] and Caesar[5] were three Reading soldiers named Freeman. Jonas was 18 years old in December of 1780 when he received a bonus from the town of Reading, enlisting for a three-year term as part of the town's commitment. A January 7, 1781, list described Doss as 32 years old, 5 feet 6 inches tall, with black complexion and "wool" hair.

Sharper[6] and Cato Freeman[7] both served from Stoneham. Cato was 30 years old and 5 feet 5 inches tall when he arrived at Fishkill to serve a term of nine months. Sharper's list of service starts in July of 1780, when he was 30. He was discharged in December and enlisted again in April of 1782. His occupation was listed as farmer and laborer.

Tewksbury—Two towns claim Prince Frie

Black patriot Prince Frie was claimed by both Andover and Tewksbury, but a military ruling credited his service to Tewksbury.[1]

Westford—Bason shows courage in Bunker Hill battle

Caesar Bason, a freeman who owned property, was one of very few blacks in Westford, Mass., in 1775. He was a private and had 12 days of service in Captain Jonathan Minot's company.[1]

Bason received pay for his service for Westford at the Concord alarm on April 19, and he was among a group of 14 Westford men at Bunker (Breed's) Hill in June of 1775.[2] According to one story, Bason discovered that his powder was nearly gone during the battle in Charlestown. He put in his last charge and yelled, "Now Caesar, give them one more." He fired, was shot, and fell back into the trench.[3] Minute Man National Park ranger and historian Mark Nichipor said records show that Bason was captured during the battle and died of his wounds while a prisoner of war.[4]

Woburn—Isaac Barbadoes earns freedom for fighting

Isaac Barbadoes of Woburn served in Captain Edmund Munroe's company, Colonel Timothy Bigelow's regiment, from April 10 to December 1777.[1] He was to earn his freedom for his military duty, but he died before his term was completed. His wages went to his mother, Lois, his legal heir. An April 1778 letter concerning the pay owed Barbadoes and due his mother confirms that he was actually released from his master prior to joining Munroe's company.[2]

The descriptive list of men raised in Middlesex County identifies Cato Wyman as a laborer, 29 years old, with black hair, eyes, and complexion. Shortly after reporting, Wyman was declared unfit for duty because, according to the record, he was "an idiot and subject to fits."[3]

National Park Service project identifies more patriots of color

The list of minority men who fought the British on April 19, 1775, and/or at the Battle of Bunker Hill is growing, thanks to a National Park Service Patriots of Color project. Historian and genealogist George Quintal reports that the latest additions to the list of men of color who served in one or both of these battles include four Massachusetts soldiers—Briny Greasier of Framingham, Caesar Wallace, who enlisted from Newbury, Caesar Wetherbee of Stow, and Porter Cuddy, who enlisted from Sudbury. Quintal also reports that Ezra Fuller, who was born in Lynn, Mass., and moved to New Ipswich, N.H., was 18 years old when he enlisted from New Ipswich.

The information gathered by Quintal will be used to create a database of patriots of color in action either on April 19, 1775, or at Bunker Hill. Quintal's work is a joint project of the Minute Man National Historical Park and the Boston National Historical Park.

Appendix B
Minuteman area Black Patriots' Trail

In the Boston area, Revolutionary War history can sometimes be found around the corner, in the back yard, or at the town common. The following list of markers and sites with ties to patriots of color in Lexington, Concord, and other nearby communities is a starting point for retracing the steps that soldiers traveled more than two centuries ago. Some sites are areas where these men once lived. Others honor their accomplishments or mark their final resting places.

This listing is intended to encourage readers in any area or state to look around their communities and create their own black patriots' trails.

• **Andover**—The gravestone of Pomp Lovejoy, who died at age 102, in 1826, is in the burial ground of South Church, 141 Central Street. Look on the left about 30 paces from the School Street entrance.

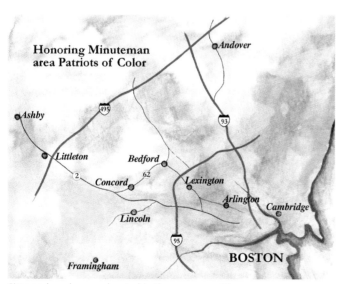

Sites and markers are located in these communities.

• **Andover**—Pomps Pond is named for Pomp Lovejoy, a freed slave who responded to the April 19, 1775, alarm. Lovejoy once built a cabin near the pond and fished and farmed in this part of Andover. The pond, off Abbot Street, is now the site of a popular town beach.

• **Arlington**—The Old Men of Menotomy marker, outside the First Parish Unitarian Universalist Church, on Mass. Ave., honors the bravery of a band of elderly men led by biracial David Lamson. Lamson and the elderly gentlemen known as the Old Men of Menotomy ambushed and captured British supply wagons headed for Lexington on April 19, 1775.

- **Arlington**—Black patriots Cuff Whittemore and Cato Wood participated in fighting near the Jason Russell House, site of the bloodiest battle of April 19, 1775. Visitors today can tour the farmhouse at 7 Jason Street, touch a bullet hole left during the clash, and visit the Arlington Historical Society's adjoining Smith Museum.

- **Ashby**—Prince Estabrook's grave site was marked in 1930, a century after his death. It is located at the rear of the First Parish Unitarian Universalist Church cemetery, off Route 119, in Ashby Center.

- **Bedford**—The African Reservation is in the northeast corner of the Old Burying Ground on Springs Road. A stone marks the common burial site of black patriots Caesar Jones, Cambridge Moore, Caesar Prescott, and about a dozen other African Americans. The town's fourth black Revolutionary soldier, Peter Freeman, is buried in Bedford's Shawsheen Cemetery.

- **Cambridge**— The remains of two Cambridge soldiers of color, Cato Stedman and Neptune Frost, are in the Old Burying Ground in Harvard Square. A blue oval plaque on the side of the cemetery facing Christ Church confirms that this is the final resting place of these Revolutionary War soldiers. The exact locations of the burial sites in the cemetery have not been identified.

- **Concord**—Meriam's Corner, at the intersection of Lexington and Old Bedford roads, marks the start of the five-mile Battle Road Trail, on which African-American soldiers, including Peter Salem of Framingham and Pomp Blackman of Lexington, fought with white colonists against His Majesty's retreating troops. This walking and bicycle path, within Minute Man National Historical Park, runs through parts of Concord, Lincoln, and Lexington. It passes the restored Hartwell Tavern and includes portions of the actual route that Regulars, militia, and minutemen traveled in 1775.

- **Concord**—Minute Man National Historical Park's North Bridge Visitor Center sits above the battle site, where Caesar Bason of Westford was among the colonial militia men who confronted the Regulars on April 19, 1775.

Along the Battle Road Trail in Minute Man National Historical Park

- **Concord**—The Hill Burying Ground, in Concord Center near Monument Square, is the final resting place of John Jack, a Concord slave who, in the years leading up to the Revolution, bought his freedom and a four-acre farm. Jack worked winters as a shoemaker. He died in 1773. His gravestone, a copy of the original marker, contains an epitaph written by Tory Daniel Bliss to tweak the Whigs' consciences and reads, in part: "God wills us free; man wills us slaves. I will as God wills. God's will be done."

- **Framingham**—The grave of black patriot Peter Salem, who fought on the afternoon of April 19, 1775, and at Bunker Hill and Saratoga, is located at the rear of the Old Burying Ground on Main Street. This cemetery is near Buckminster Square, the site of Framingham's Minuteman statue.

Peter Salem's burial site

- **Framingham**—A bridge on Old Connecticut Path was named in honor of Crispus Attucks on March 5, 2000. The dedication pays tribute to the runaway slave, the first of five civilians killed by British troops in the 1770 Boston Massacre. The bridge is close to the Wayland line, near land once owned by Attucks's master, Deacon William Brown.

- **Lexington**—A diorama of the Battle of Lexington on display at the Lexington Visitor Center is a historic representation of the scene on Lexington Common, April 19, 1775. The display includes the figure of Prince Estabrook with a shoulder wound.

- **Lexington**—A Revolutionary War memorial near the Buckman Tavern honors the members of Captain Parker's Lexington company on duty the morning of April 19, 1775. Look on the back of the monument for Prince Estabrook's name.

- **Lexington**—Each year the Lexington Minute Men reenact the 1775 encounter on the Battle Green. For the exact date of this piece of living history and other Patriot's Day events in Concord, Lincoln, and Lexington, contact the town celebrations committees or Chambers of Commerce, Minute Man National Historical Park, or the Lexington Historical Society.

- **Lexington-Lincoln line**—The Minute Man National Historical Park Visitor Center, off Route 2A, offers exhibits, events, and a multimedia presentation on the Battle of Lexington and Concord. The Battle Road Trail can be accessed from the Visitor Center.

- **Lincoln**—Scippio Brister's grave is in the Precinct Burial Ground of the Lexington Road cemetery, just below a ridge where five British soldiers were buried. Lexington Road runs from Route 2 to Trapelo Road. From Route 2, look for the cemetery on your right. On entering, turn left at the first fork. Brister's marker will be on the right, across the road from a section of old gravestones.

- **Littleton**—A Revolutionary War monument in Liberty Square, at the intersection of Taylor Road and Hill Street, includes the name of the black patriot Scipio [Chase].

Additional resources in Boston:

- To check out sites honoring black patriots in Boston, contact the Boston Museum of Afro-American History.

- For information about the Bunker Hill monument and the Boston Black Heritage walking tour, contact Boston National Historical Park.

Appendix C
Remembering black patriots

In Washington, D.C., plans are underway to fund and build a memorial to honor the estimated 5,000 forgotten enslaved and freed men and women of African heritage who participated in the pursuit of freedom during the Revolutionary War era. Congress has approved a location for the Black Revolutionary War Patriots Memorial near the Vietnam Memorial on the National Mall to honor African Americans and the fight for independence.

The purpose of this national memorial is to raise awareness of black patriots' efforts and to promote the spirit of American freedom, diversity, and equality. Sculptor Ed Dwight, the first African American to be trained as an astronaut, has created the memorial design. A granite walkway leads visitors through a pair of curved and sloping walls to a circular plaza. The southern wall is dark granite, engraved with the words of freed slave and Boston poet Phillis Wheatley. The memorial's northern wall features a curving bronze sculpture, rising east to west, ranging from three feet to seven and a half feet in height. The first section reveals vague hints of figures that gradually expand in size and detail until they emerge into life-size figures. The sculpture chronicles the war and ends with a black family standing proud, facing the Lincoln Memorial. This is to symbolize that although the country had achieved independence, black people would have to wait for their personal freedom.

The financial goal of the Black Patriots Foundation is to raise 12 million dollars to build the memorial and to establish an educational component. Success depends upon contributions from citizens, foundations, and corporations. The Black Patriots Foundation is also selling commemorative coins, produced by the United States Mint, depicting Crispus Attucks, the first man to die in the Boston Massacre.

For information on the memorial, contact the Black Patriots Foundation in Washington, D.C., or visit the foundation's Web site at www.blackpatriots.org.

Black history comes alive at Williamsburg

L iving history programs at Virginia's Colonial Williamsburg are helping visitors today understand the struggles of slaves and their families during the Revolutionary War era. "The Sword is Drawn" is one of a series of historical dramas regularly presented at the reconstructed eighteenth-century outdoor museum. It is based on royal governor and slaveowner Lord Dunmore's offer to give freedom to slaves who agree to fight for the Crown. The reenactment depicts the reaction to Dunmore's controversial November 1775 proclamation.

Another of the Williamsburg reenactments, "To Run or Stay," focuses on a traumatic day in the lives of slaves Peter and Sarah Southall, a young couple expecting their first child. Visitors agonize along with the Southalls over the complex life or death decisions the couple must make.

Onlookers often get drawn into the drama and emotion of the stories as they unfold, according to Harvey Bakari, manager of African-American programs at Colonial Williamsburg. These carefully researched dramas don't pull punches, Bakari says. They portray the slaves' powerful longings for freedom and dignity and show the clashing interests of the white and black communities, as patrols try to prevent slaves from escaping.

For more information on these reenactments and other programs that explore the impact of slavery on the lives of all colonial Virginians, contact Colonial Williamsburg, in Williamsburg, Va.

In this Colonial Williamsburg reenactment, Peter, a runaway slave, listens to see if it is safe to proceed on his journey to freedom.

Endnotes*

Introduction

[1] Under Chapter 130, the Acts of 1894, the Massachusetts Legislature designated April 19 as Patriot's Day, honoring the 1775 Battle of Lexington and Concord. Today this state holiday is officially celebrated the third Monday in April. On April, 19, 1894, the governor and other officials attended events in Concord and Lexington where the festivities included a procession, band concert, banquet, and ball. As a lasting tribute, streets and roads from the center of Dorchester through Boston, Cambridge, Arlington, and Lexington were combined in 1894 as Massachusetts Avenue.

[2] While Captain Parker and his men did not intend a confrontation on the morning April 19, 1775, they were angered by the Regulars' demand to disarm. Historians generally agree that the 5 a.m. clash that took place after a mysterious shot was fired was the Revolutionary War's first organized encounter between British soldiers and a colonial militia unit. On page 21 of *April 19,1775, A Historiographical Study* (Minuteman National Historical Park, 1987), retired Minute Man National Historical Park historian Douglas Sabin states, "The Americans who died on Lexington Common were the first fatalities of the war that resulted in the independence of the United States." In *The Negro in the American Revolution* (Chapel Hill, NC, 1961), author Benjamin Quarles writes that the Lexington militiamen were, "the first to enter the fray." If the soldiers who died in that clash are the war's first fatalities, it follows that, as the only black man recorded as a participant, Prince Estabrook can be considered the first black American soldier in the Revolution. In a project coordinated by Charles Price, the Lexington Minute Men placed a plaque at Arlington National Cemetery on June 10, 2000, honoring the eight men killed in action at dawn April 19, 1775, during the first encounter of the American Revolution.

Keeping the story alive

[1] The modern-day Lexington Minute Men company is an educational and ceremonial organization, following in the tradition of Captain Parker's company, which was organized Dec. 13, 1773.

[2] Lexington, along with other Massachusetts Bay communities, had its own militia company or training band. As tensions with Great Britain rose, the Provincial Congress created a Committee of Safety in the fall of 1774 and suggested that existing local militia companies form new elite groups, comprising about a fourth of the training band, which could assemble on virtually a minute's notice. Local alarm companies of older men were also recommended to lend support in emergencies. Key Lexington records for this period disappeared, but it appears officials kept troops in one company. Although the men on the Common April 19, 1775, were not technically "minutemen," they had trained regularly and many had military experience from the French and Indian Wars. From Charles Hudson's *History of Lexington* (Boston: Houghton Mifflin, 1868), vol. I, 1913, pp. 421–33; and David Hackett Fischer's *Paul Revere's Ride*, (New York: Oxford University Press, 1994), pp. 151–55.

[3] Descriptions of the Patriot's Day reenactment were written from the author's personal observation and information supplied by Charles Price and George Gabriel, a modern-day Lexington Minute Man who portrays Captain Parker.

Spelling, capitalization, punctuation, and misspellings contained in original documents have been retained, except when changes were needed for clarity.

4 While part of this quotation is confirmed in the testimony of members of Parker's company, serious doubts have been raised about the accuracy of the complete quotation. See Harold Murdock's *The Nineteenth of April 1775*, 1925, p. 39.

Looking back

1 Edwin B. Worthen, *A Calendar History of Lexington, Massachusetts 1620–1946*, Lexington, 1946, p.31. The 1775 minutes of the Lexington Board of Selectmen, excluding missing sections, are stored in the Lexington Town Clerk's Office. A typed transcript is in the Lexington Historical Society's collection.

2 Hudson, *History of Lexington*, vol. I, pp. 421–26.

3 Fischer, pp. 327–28. Depositions given by some Lexington militiamen in 1775, are reprinted on pp. 663–67 in *The Journals of Each Provincial Congress of Massachusetts in 1774 and 1775 and of the Committee of Safety with an Appendix,* edited by William Lincoln, Boston, 1838. They can be compared with testimony at the time of the 50th anniversary, in Elias Phinney's *History of the Battle at Lexington*, (Boston, 1825) pp. 31–40.

4 Sabin, p. 21.

5 Joseph's name is not included in the first list of participants in the April 19 dawn confrontation, but it appears in a later report. He is also recorded as serving with the Lexington militia in Cambridge on May 11–15, 1775. He was said to be 17 years old on April 19, 1775. An 1826 letter Joseph sent to the Concord minister stated: "After more than half a century, to the best of my recollection, I would inform you and others, that I stood in the ranks, on the parade, till Captain Parker ordered us to disperse, and till the British came nigh to us and began to fire upon us, when I left the ranks. At that time, all was confusion and distress. I did not see any one of the Lexington company fire upon the British, nor was there any order for it, that I can recollect, from our captain. But from the statement of the committee and the testimony of some worthy individuals, I believe a few guns did return the fire on the British Troops, before they left the parade, where the company was placed, on that never to be forgotten morning." (From Hudson's *History of Lexington*, pp. 421–25, and Ezra Ripley's *A History of the Fight at Concord on the 19th of April, 1775* (Concord, 1827), p. 44.

6 Interviews with Concord Minute Men historian D. Michael Ryan, Feb. 25, 2000, and July 13, 2000.

7 Ibid.

8 Fischer, pp. 320–24 and Minute Man National Historical Park (MMNHP) informational brochure on the park and Battle Road Trail, 1991.

9 Quarles, *The Negro in the American Revolution*, p. 10.

10 *Massachusetts Soldiers and Sailors of American Revolutionary War,* vol II, p. 283 and vol. XIV, p. 14. Records compiled from the archives by the Secretary of the Commonwealth, Boston: 1899. Copies in Cary Memorial and other libraries.

11 Fischer, p. 242.

12 Ibid., pp. 320–24.

13 Historian George Quintal is conducting research for a National Park Service project.

"When liberty is the prize"

1 Photos showing the statue and the text of the plaque featuring Joseph Warren's quotation are in the collection of the Society for the Preservation of New England Antiquities (SPNEA) in Boston, Mass. .

2 Confirmed by Roxbury Latin School staff, Boston, Mass.

3 Charles Price, interviews by author in Lexington between Dec. 29, 1994 and June 15, 2000, and in Roxbury on March 25, 2000.

4 Ibid.

From farm field to battlefield

1 Hudson, 1913, vol. 1, p. 31.
2 Edwin B. Worthen, *Tracing the Past in Lexington, Massachusetts*, (New York, 1998), pp. 7–8.
3 Ibid., p. 11.
4 Canavan, vol. 3, p. 426.
5 Massachusetts Judicial Archives, Middlesex County Probate Files, #7036, Joseph Estabrook III, 1740.
6 *History of the Town of Lexington*, vol. I, 1913, Hudson, p. 481. The Slave Census 1754–55, in the Massachusetts State Archives, Boston, Mass., shows 24 negroes in Lexington.
7 Hudson's *History of Lexington*, 1913, vol. II, p. 62, also Lexington Board of Selectmen's minutes, March 5, 1781.
8 Lexington Board of Selectmen minutes, March 27, 1769.
9 Canavan, vol. 3, p. 471.
10 Based on information in *Massachusetts Soldiers and Sailors,* vol V, pp. 155, 157, 389, and 392. There is no record of Prince Estabrook's birth. In tax rolls and on muster lists, his name is spelled many different ways, including: Estabrook, Easterbrooks, Esterbrooks, Estabrooke, and Efterbrook. Misspellings during this period were rampant, and substituting an "f" for an "s" was common.
11 Staples, "The Existence and the Extinction of Slavery in Massachusetts," *Proceedings of the Lexington Historical Society*, vol. IV, 1912, p.54. 1902 paper by the Reverend C. A. Staples, pastor, First Parish Unitarian Church Lexington from 1881–1904 and Lexington Historical Society historian.
12 Edward Ball, *Slaves in the Family* (New York: Ballantine Books, 1999), p. 52.
13 Staples, *Proceedings of the Lexington Historical Society*, vol. IV, p.53.
14 Eusebious Esterbrook was the master of the ship *Eagle of Biddeford* (now *Maine*), licensed Dec. 10, 1687, to sail from Boston for Barbadoes, but no ties have been found as yet to the Estabrooks of Lexington. From Massachusetts Archives Collection, (SC1-45x) vol. 7, p. 39.
15 Robert A. Gross, *The Minutemen and Their World,* (1976, New York), p. 90, and Hudson's *History of Lexington,* (1913), vol. I, pp. 63–65.
16 Lexington Board of Selectmen minutes, May 1753. One of many other examples of citizens vouching for persons entering town was recorded in the Lexington Board of Selectmen's minutes, February 12, 1772. Samuel Bridge informed the board: "I have taken into my House to reside with me one Robert Tulep [Tulip], a Negro man. He came to me on the first of February Instant, he Came last from Boston, but is property and Inhabitant of Marboro. his Circumstances are Low."
17 Massachusetts Judicial Archives, Middlesex County Probate Files, #7033, Joseph Estabrook II, 1733.
18 Canavan, vol. 3, pp. 411, 502.
19 Canavan, vol. 3, p. 432.
20 Estabrook histories in Concord Free Library special collections: *Genealogy of the Anglo-Dutch Estabrooks Family of the Saint John River, New Brunswick,* by Florence C. Estabrooks, p. 8, and *The Estabrook's Family in Concord, Massachusetts and on the Saint John River, New Brunswick, Canada,* vol. I, p. 38.
21 Hudson's *History of Lexington*, vol. I, p. 553.
22 Canavan, vol. 3, p. 471.
23 *Journals of Each Provincial Congress of Massachusetts in 1774 and 1775 and of the Committee of Safety*, William Lincoln, ed., Boston, 1837. Claims ranged from Estabrook's 12 pounds to Joseph Loring's 720 pounds. Also Hudson, vol. 1, 1913, p. 174.

Fighting for liberty . . . and liberation

1 *Massachusetts Soldiers and Sailors*, vol. V, pp. 155, 157, 389, and 392.
2 *Massachusetts Soldiers and Sailors*, vol. V, p. 156 and Hudson's *History of Lexington*, vol. 1, p. 427.
3 Muster rolls of the Revolution, state militia, Massachusetts Archives Collection, File F, vol. 55, p. 50.

4 Canavan, vol. 2, p. 271.

5 Ibid., pp. 273–74.

6 Telephone interviews with Fort Ticonderoga Museum curator Christopher Fox, Jan. 5, 2000, and Aug. 14, 2000.

7 Canavan, vol. 2, p. 274. Letter in Lexington Historical Society archives.

8 Ibid.

9 *Massachusetts Soldiers and Sailors*, vol. V, p. 389.

10 *Massachusetts Soldiers and Sailors*, vol. V, contains two different descriptions of Estabrook. While there is no way to know which is correct, he was described as a tall man who took his place in the second (taller) line of the militia company on April 19, 1775, according to town legend.

11 Research of Henry Cooke IV, costume historian of Randolph, Mass. Telephone interview, Sept. 21, 2000, and information in *Collectors Illustrated Encyclopedia of the American Revolution,* by George Newmann (2nd), p. 55, and *Uniforms of the Continental Army*, Philip Katcher, published by George Shumway, York, Pa., 1981, p. 104.

12 Robert K. Wright Jr., *The Continental Army*. (Washington, D.C.: U.S. Army Center of Military History, 1989), p. 206.

13 Telephone interviews with Alan Amonine, Senior Special Collections Librarian at the U.S. Military Academy Library at West Point, New York, Jan. 5, 2000, Jan. 16, 1996, and March 7, 2000 respectively.

14 Lincoln Diamant, *Chaining the Hudson*, p. 3.

15 Muster roll, Oct. 14, 1783, on microfilm at the National Archives and Records Administration, Northeast Region, Waltham, Mass., vol. 3, p. 132, and Wright, p. 206.

After the war

1 "A Sketch of the History of Lexington Common," read Oct. 12, 1886, C. A. Staples. *Proceedings*, vol. 1, p. 25.

2 U. S. Federal Census, 1790 for Massachusetts. The National Archives, Northeast Region, Waltham, Mass.

3 Eighteenth-century tax rolls, Assessors Records, Town of Lexington, Assessor's Office.

4 "Washington's Visit to Lexington," *Proceedings of the Lexington Historical Society*, 1890, vol. 1, page liii.

5 Flip, an alcoholic beverage made of hot, spiced wine whipped with egg, was a favorite in taverns, including Buckman Tavern. According to legend, it was the drink some militiamen used to warm themselves and boost their courage, as they waited in the early morning hours of April 19, 1775.

6 Canavan, vol. 1, p. 125.

7 Staples, *Slavery in Lexington*, vol. IV, Slavery, p. 54.

8 Benjamin Estabrook, Value of His Estate, 1803, probate document, Massachusetts Judicial Archives, Middlesex County Probate Files, 1643–1871, and Worthen's *Tracing the Past*, p. 11.

9 Francis H. Brown, M.D., *A Copy of Epitaphs in the Old Burying-Grounds of Lexington, Massachusetts,* The Lexington Historical Society, 1905, p. 33.

10 Hudson, *History*, vol. ll, 1913, p. 63.

11 Lexington Board of Selectmen minutes, from June 11, 1802 to Nov. 25, 1805.

12 Lexington Board of Selectmen minutes, April 2, 1804. (Hog reeves—the persons in each town charged with assessing damages and settling claims on damages by hogs. Major tasks were preventing damages inflicted by stray hogs or estimating damages attributed to them. Selectmen voted whether hogs should be penned up or allowed to run free in a particular year.)

13 Kidder and Gould, *History of New Ipswich from First Grant in MDCCXXXVI to the Present Time,* 1852 Boston., pp. 235, 387.

14 Worthen, *Tracing Our Past,* pp.11–12.

15 From a handwritten letter in Cary Memorial Library's Edwin B. Worthen Collection from Worthen to Donald E. Nickerson, chairman of the Board of Selectmen, dated Aug. 15, 1951.
16 Original deed in Middlesex South Registry of Deeds, East Cambridge, Mass.
17 Worthen, *Tracing the Past*, pp. 12,13.
18 Lexington Board of Selectmen minutes, 1802 to 1815.
19 Canavan, vol. 3, p. 433.
20 Attai and his wife sold church pew Number 17, on the lower floor in the meeting house, to Phineas Lawrence for $120. The transaction took place April 21, 1807, but was not recorded until the Feb. 29, 1808 Selectmen's meeting, where it appears in the minutes.
21 Hudson, *History*, 1913, vol. II. p. 63.
22 Worthen, *Tracing our Past*, p. 15.
23 Staples, *Slavery in Lexington, Proceedings*, vol. IV, p. 54.
24 Sons of the American Revolution (Massachusetts SAR) bulletin, Nov. 1930, pp. 7–8.
25 *Cemetery Records of Ashby, Middlesex County, Massachusetts to 1865*, compiled by Arthur D. Fiske (Seattle, 1964).
26 Massachusetts SAR Bulletin, Nov. 30, 1930.
27 Although the psalm book has not been tested to confirm its age and authenticity, Lexington Historical Society Director George Comtois said the book's appearance and condition are consistent with books of the late eighteenth century, and he sees no reason to doubt Stetson's claim.
28 Worthen, *Calendar History,* pp. 34, 36.
29 Church Records, First Parish Church of Watertown, record book, 1668–1818, Massachusetts Historical Society, Boston.

Prejudice, controversy, and hope

1 *The Negro in the American Revolution*, Quarles, p. ix, *Black Courage*, p. xxix.
2 Ibid, p.71.
3 *In Hope of Liberty,* by Horton & Horton, pp. 24–5, 1997. Also *The Negro in Colonial New England*, pp. 212–13, 282, 283, 326–30.
4 *The Negro American: A Documentary History,* Lesliel H. Fishel Jr., and Benjamin Quarles, pp. 13, 14.
5 *The Negro in the American Revolution*, Quarles, p. 15.
6 Quarles, p. 14.
7 Thomas to John Adams, Oct. 24, 1775, quoted in the *Papers of John Adams, Vol. 3*. Robert J. Taylor, ed. Cambridge, Mass.:Belknap Press, 1979, p. 239..
8 Quarles, p. 72.
9 Ibid.
10 Sidney Kaplan and Emma Nogrady Kaplan, and *The Negro Presence in the Era of the American Revolution, 1770–1800* (Amherst: U Massachusetts Press, 1989), pp. 73, 74, 174–80.
11 Quarles, pp. 16, 174–80.
12 Ibid, p. 17
13 Ibid., pp. 16–17.
14 Ibid., p. 54.
15 Quarles, pp. 73–80, and Kaplan, pp. 64–65.
16 Quoted in Quarles, pp. 62–63.
17 Kaplan, p. 34. Kaplan also notes that von Closen's journal discusses a meeting with a slave ship under an Austrian flag. Of these ships, von Closen wrote, the negroes are treated "worse than beasts. . . there is a chain which crosses from one side to the other, to which they are all attached, two by two, except for a few . . . All these unfortunate beings are naked, and at the least movement that does not

suit the Captain, they are beaten to a pulp." He added that about a fifth of the slaves usually die from sickness or despair during the two- to three-month voyage.

18 Quarles, p. 53.

19 Brown, Abram English, *History of the Town of Bedford, Massachusetts from its Earliest Settlement to the Year of Our Lord, 1891*. Bedford, Mass., 1891, p. 32.

20 Quarles, p. xxvii.

21 Ibid., p. 74.

22 Ibid.

23 Kaplan, p. 27.

24 Zilversmit, Arthur, *The First Emancipation: The Abolition of Slavery in the North*, (University of Chicago Press, 1967), p. 37.

25 A state Supreme Court decision rendered by Chief Justice William Cushing in *Commonwealth v. Jennison*, 1783, with all judges concurring, confirmed the 1780 declaration of rights. It dealt a death blow to slavery in Massachusetts, allowing upwards of 4,000 slaves to obtain their freedom. The decision's conclusion, in part, states: "But whatever sentiments have formerly prevailed . . . a different idea has taken place with the people of America, more favorable to the natural rights of mankind and that natural, innate love of Liberty with which Heaven, without regard to color, complexion, or shape of noses, or features, has inspired all the human race . . . And upon this ground, our Constitution of Government sets out with declaring that all men are born free and equal and that every subject is entitled to liberty and to have it guarded by the laws, as well as life and property, and, in short, is totally repugnant to the idea of being born slaves. This being the case, I think the idea of slavery is inconsistent with our conduct and Constitution, and there can be no such thing as perpetual servitude of a rational creature unless his liberty is forfeited by criminal conduct or given up by personal consent or contract." From Staples, *Proceedings*, vol. IV, pp. 59–60.

26 Sabin, "The Role of Blacks in the Battle of 1775," circa 1992, MMNHP, and Wallace, Teresa, paper on Peter Salem.

27 Staples, *Proceedings of the Lexington Historical Society*, Slavery, v. IV, p. 64.

28 Zilversmit, p. 226.

29 Ibid., p. 228–29.

30 Calloway, Colin G., *The American Revolution in Indian Country* (Cambridge University Press, 1995), pp. 90–95.

31 Ibid., p. 96.

32 Ibid., p. 103.

Progress "deadly slow"

1 The following is an example of an eighteenth-century slave transaction. The document, dated June 5, AD 1752, with witnesses Benjamin Brown and Eunice Anger, is in the Lexington Historical Society archives.

Bill of Sale of a Negro, Pompey, June 5, 1752. Sold by Ruth Bowman, widow, to William Reed, both of Lexington

"Know yee that I Ruth Bowman of Lexington in ye County of Middlesex in ye province of Massachusetts Bay in New England & widdow woman, for & in consideration of Fifty Three pound, six shillings & eight pence Lawful mony of New England to me in hand well & truly Paid by William Reed of ye aforesd. Town & County __ the receipt whereof at the executing of these presents I acknowledge until my full satisfaction & content have according to ye Powers in me _____ by the Donation of my hand: husband Francis Bowman Esq. late of Lexington deceased giving granted aliened, & confirmed, & do by these Presents give grant, Bargain, sell, aliend Convey, & Confirm unto ye sd. William Reed, the whole of my Right Title, Interest, Claim, Property, & Demand of __ & to my negro man called Pompey, to have & to hold the said Pompey During ye whole Term of his natural Life to him ye sd: William Reed his heirs Exed: Adminet; & assigns, & to their sole benefitt & behooff for ever. and I the sd. Ruth Bowman do hereby convenant & engage, that at ye _____ of these Presents, I am the sole & Proper owner of ye said Negro, & have in my Self good Right full power & Lawful Authority to Convey the said Negro for Life as aforesd . . . .

"For ye said William Reed his heirs & assigns at all times for ever hereafter, to have, hold, use, Improve, Imploy, & enjoy ye Service of ye said negro, peaceably & quietly without the Denial or Contradiction of me ye sd. Ruth Bowman, my heirs or assigns, or any other under me or by act neglect, default or Procurement, & this Conveyance of ye sd: negro as aforesd, I will for ever warrant & defend from ye challenges or claims of all Persons whatsoever."

[2] While slaves held in Lexington were servants in most cases, at least one family engaged in the slave trade, according to Hudson, p. 482, 1913 edition, vol. 1. Hudson wrote that, in 1727, the slavetrader (identified only by first name), reportedly offered a reward for a runaway described this way: "He speaks very good English, is about 26 years of age, had no hat on, but had a horse lock about one of his legs; and was lately the property of John Muzzey, of Mendon."

[3] Massachusetts Judicial Archives, Middlesex County Probate Files, #7026, John Esterbrook [sic], 1742.

[4] Price, interview.

[5] In a letter sent from the Adjutant General's office in Washington D.C., dated July 10, 1929, Robert C. Cotton, Major, Infantry D.O.L., writes to the quartermaster General, 3rd battalion Massachusetts General Guard, explaining the history of Company L, 372nd Infantry of the 93rd Division. It was a segregated black unit that served principally with the French 157th Division during World War I and participated in the Meuse-Argonne campaign. The unit was honored by the French government for its courageous service and members earned the right to wear the French Croix de Guerre. The letter further states that "it is recommended that the 3rd Battalion, 372nd infantry Massachusetts [National Guard, a descendant of the 372nd], be authorized to bear on its color, a streamer in the colors of the ribbon of the French Croix de Guerre with the inscription 'Meuse Argonne.' "

[6] Price, interview.

[7] Ibid.

Appendix A—Other unsung heroes

Andover

[1] Kaplan, p. 23 and Massachusetts Archives, Document 180:241.

[2] *Massachusetts Soldiers and Sailors*, 561, vol. XII, and Quarles, p. 11.

[3] *Massachusetts Soldiers and Sailors*, vol. XIII, p. 685.

[4] *Massachusetts Soldiers and Sailors*, vol. VIII, p. 811.

[5] *Massachusetts Soldiers and Sailors*, vol. V, p. 892–93.

[6] *Massachusetts Soldiers and Sailors*, vol. VI, pp. 34, 211, and Quarles, p. 53.

[7] *Massachusetts Soldiers and Sailors*, vol. IX, p. 996.

[8] Fuess, Claude M. *Andover: Symbol of New England*, The Andover Historical Society and the North Andover Historical Society, 1959, p. 311.

[9] Richardson, Eleanor Motley. *Andover: A Century of Change 1896–1996*, The Andover Historical Society, 1995, p. 210.

[10] Quarles, p. 53.

[11] Fuess, p. 312.

[12] *Massachusetts Soldiers and Sailors*, vol. VI, p. 34; vol. III, p. 211 (as Cato of Andover) and vol. V, p. 893.

Arlington

1 Sabin, "The Role of Blacks in the Battle of April 19, 1775," pp. 1, 2.
2 Ibid.
3 Ibid.
4 Paul Hogman, past captain of Menotomy Minute Men, telephone interview, Feb. 11, 2000.
5 *Massachusetts Soldiers and Sailors*, vol. IX, p. 452.
6 Hogman.
7 *Massachusetts Soldiers and Sailors*, vol. XVII, Whittemore, p. 264.
8 *Massachusetts Soldiers and Sailors*, vol. XVII, p. 721.
9 Kaplan, p. 20.
10 Charles Parker, *Town of Arlington, Past and Present*. Arlington, Mass.: C. S. Parker Sons, 1907. p. 197.
11 Revolutionary War Pension and Bounty Land Warrant Application files, 1800–1900, series M804, Roll 2469. National Archives, Northeast Region. Revolutionary War pension claims, S. 33896, based on military service of Cuff Whittemore.

Bedford

1 Abram E. Brown, *History of the Town of Bedford, Massachusetts from its Earliest Settlement to the Year of Our Lord, 1891*. Bedford, Mass., 1891, pp. 27–34, 67, 92. Also *The History of Middlesex County, Massachusetts,* vol. 2, p. 837. Philadelphia: D. H. Hurd, 1890.
2 *Massachusetts Soldiers & Sailors*, vol. VIII, p. 903.
3 *Massachusetts Soldiers & Sailors*, vol. X, p. 916.
4 *Massachusetts Soldiers & Sailors*, vol. VII, p. 750.
5 Louise K. Brown, *A Revolutionary Town* (Canaan, N. H.: Phoenix Publishers, 1975), pp. 212, 285, 296. Published in cooperation with The Bedford Historical Society.
6 Brown, Abram English, p. 32.
7 *Vital Records of Bedford, to the year 1850*, p. 58.
8 Ibid., pp. 121, 142.
9 Bedford Historical Society Research Project: John Brown, Dana Morse, Helen Nowers, Eunice Puzzo, and Robert Slechta, *The Old Burying Ground Gravestone Survey, Map, and Data Bases, Bedford, Mass., 1993–1995.*
10 In 1975, Bedford residents Rachel Murphy and Martha Smith, assisted by Irene Parker and the late Ina Mansur, Bedford historian, researched the contributions of these eighteenth-century black soldiers and other African-American residents. The women presented the results of their efforts to the town as a Bicentennial gift in January of 1976. It is located in the Bedford Free Library's Bedford Collection.

Cambridge

1 *Massachusetts Soldiers and Sailors,* vol. II, p. 283.
2 *Massachusetts Soldiers and Sailors,* vol. XIV, p. 900.
3 *Massachusetts Soldiers and Sailors,* vol. VI, p. 121.

Chelmsford and Dracut

1 Franklin A. Dorman, *Twenty Families of Color in Massachusetts, 1742–1998*, (Boston: New England Historic and Genealogical Society), pp. 272–73.
2 *Massachusetts Soldiers and Sailors*, vol IX, p. 725.
3 Dorman, *Twenty Families*, 1742–1998, p. 273.
4 Research by Martha Mayo, director, Center for Lowell History at UMass, Lowell, for Profiles in Courage exhibit, African Americans in Lowell.
5 Dorman, *Twenty Families*, p. 273.

6 *History of Middlesex County (1890),* pp. 310–11.
7 Research by Martha Mayo, director, Center for Lowell History at UMass, Lowell, for Profiles in Courage exhibit, African Americans in Lowell.
8 Ibid.
9 Confirmed by curator of DuSable Museum of African-American History, 740 E. 56th Place, Chicago 60637.
10 "Echoes of the Underground Railroad" by Tatsha Robertson, *Boston Globe,* Feb. 22, 1999, p. 1. Phyllis Lew telephone interview, March 24, 2000.
11 Ibid.
12 Ibid.

Concord

1 *Massachusetts Soldiers and Sailors,* vol. I, pp. 676, 684.
2 *Massachusetts Soldiers and Sailors,* vol. X, p. 816.
3 Ryan, D. Michael. "Slavery and Two Fights for Freedom," *Concord Journal,* 8 Aug., 1966, p. 16.
4 Entered as Case Whiteney [sic] *Massachusetts Soldiers and Sailors,* vol. XVII, p. 159.
5 Torrey, Bradford and Francis H. Allen, eds. *The Journals of Henry D. Thoreau,* Vols. VIII–XIV (November 1855–1861), New York: Dover Publications, 1962. Feb. 18, 1858, p. 1253.
6 *Massachusetts Soldiers and Sailors,* vol. VI, p. 32.
7 Ryan, D. Michael, "Slavery and Two Fights for Freedom," *Concord Journal.*
8 Kaplan, p. 263.

Framingham

1 *Massachusetts Soldiers and Sailors,* vol. XIII, pp. 743–44, and Quarles, pp. 10, 11.
2 Extracts from Dr. Belknap's Notebooks in the Massachusetts Historical Society proceedings, 1st Ser., 14 (1876), p. 93.
3 Town Clerk's Office, Leicester, Mass.
4 Wallace, Teresa, paper on Peter Salem, June 2000.

Lexington

1 Worthen, pp. 30–8.
2 Hudson, vol. 1 (1913), p. 432.
3 Ibid.
4 *Massachusetts Soldiers and Sailors,* vol. II, p. 828 and Hudson, 1868 ed., p. 384.
5 *Massachusetts Soldiers and Sailors,* vol. II, p. 829.
6 Hudson, *History of Lexington,* vol. I, 1913, pp. 424–25.
7 Hudson, *History of Lexington,* vol. II, 1913, p. 81.
8 Hudson, vol. I, 1886, Lexington genealogy, p. 33.
9 *Massachusetts Soldiers and Sailors,* vol. II, pp. 110, 552, and Mass Rev. War Rolls, vol. 3, p. 40, National Archives, Northeast Region, R.P. 436.786.
10 The papers of Amos Fortune, Jaffrey Public Library archives in Jaffrey, N.H.
11 Munro(e) letter (May 12, 1778), Lexington Historical Society archives.
12 Hudson, 1913, vol. II, p. 489.
13 *Massachusetts Soldiers and Sailors,* vol. XVI, p. 40.
14 Ibid., vol. IV, p. 66.
15 Ibid., vol. V, p. 728.
16 Ibid., vol. XVI, p. 128.
17 Ibid., vol. XV, p. 762.

Lincoln

1 *Massachusetts Soldiers and Sailors*, vol. VIII, pp. 2, 9. Also MacLean, *A Rich Harvest*, p. 294.
2 MacLean, John, Lincoln historian, telephone interview, March 9, 2000.
3 *Massachusetts Soldiers and Sailors*, vol. IV, p. 17. Also *A Rich Harvest*, p. 294.
4 *Massachusetts Soldiers and Sailors*, vol. II, p. 338. Also *A Rich Harvest*, p. 294.
5 *Massachusetts Soldiers and Sailors*, vol. V, p. 534. Also *A Rich Harvest*, p. 294.
6 *A Rich Harvest*, p. 294

Littleton

1 *Massachusetts Soldiers and Sailors*, vol. III, pp. 366, 905.
2 *Records of Littleton, Massachusetts, Births and Deaths, from the earliest records*, 1715–1900, p. 339.

Medford

1 Kaplan, p, 28, and *Massachusetts Soldiers and Sailors*, vol. VII, p. 105.
2 Jay Griffin, Medford Historical Society president, "Prince Hall, A Man of Courage and Vision in Colonial Medford," pp. 9,10, and Quarles, pp. 43, 44.
3 *Massachusetts Soldiers and Sailors*, vol. VI, p. 49.

Reading and Stoneham

1 Quarles, p. 52.
2 *Massachusetts Soldiers and Sailors of the Revolutionary War*, vol. VI.
3 Ibid., p. 45.
4 Ibid., p. 35.
5 Ibid., p. 32.
6 Ibid., p. 51.
7 Ibid., p. 33.

Tewksbury

1 *Massachusetts Soldiers and Sailors*, vol. VI, p. 99.

Westford

1 *Massachusetts Soldiers and Sailors*, vol. I, p. 746.
2 Ryan, interview.
3 Reverend Edwin R. Hogman, *History of the Town of Westford, 1659–1883*. The Westford Town History Association, 1883, p. 113.
4 Mark Nichipor, historian and MMNHP ranger, interview, July 13, 1995.

Woburn

1 *Massachusetts Soldiers and Sailors*, vol. I, p. 583.
2 Letter in Lexington Historical Society archives.

This may certify whom it may concern that Isaac Birbadoes, (Barbadoes) a negro man that enlisted in Captain Edmund Munro's company and Col Bigelow's regiment, was legally discharged from his late master Before his first muster for the Continental Sarvis and that the mother of the adforesaid negro discharged is the legal heir being born in lawful wedlock to the wages that was due to said Negro when he was discharged and whereas hir master given hir hir time on the Condition that she will maintain hirself we think it may be of great sarvice to hir.

3 *Massachusetts Soldiers and Sailors*, vol. XVII, p. 977.

Selected bibliography

This bibliography contains the records, books, and published and unpublished accounts that I found most helpful in understanding the life and times of Prince Estabrook. Also included are materials that offer information on the lives of other patriots of color, the prejudice that was deeply ingrained in Prince Estabrook's world, and how the longing for freedom from British tyranny gradually led, in the North, to the abolition of slavery, if not of prejudice.

Federal, state, and local records and documents

Bedford Historical Society Research Project: John Brown, Dana Morse, Helen Nowers, Eunice Puzzo, and Robert Slechta, *The Old Burying Ground Gravestone Survey, Map, and Data Bases*. Bedford, Mass.: 1993–1995.

Birth, Marriage, and Death Records of the Town of Ashby, Massachusetts from 1754 to 1890. Compiled by Jeannette D. Pingrey, American Data Services, 1989, (Decorah, Iowa: The Amundson Publishing Co.).

The Book Wherein is Recorded the Births and Deaths of Those Born and Buried in the Town of New Ipswich in New Hampshire and Record of Marriages Verified. 1898. Town Clerk's Office, New Ipswich, N.H.

Brown, Francis H., M.D. *A Copy of Epitaphs in the Old Burying-Grounds of Lexington, Massachusetts*. Lexington, Mass.: The Lexington Historical Society, 1905.

Cemetery Records of Ashby, Middlesex County, Massachusetts, to 1865. Compiled by Arthur D. Fiske. Seattle: 1964.

Description of the Battle of Lexington by Lt. Mackenzie of the Royal Welsh Fusileers. *Proceedings of the Massachusetts Historical Society*, Second Series, vol. V, 1889–1890.

Estabrook family wills and estate inventories. Middlesex County Probate Files, 1643–1871 in the Massachusetts Judicial Archives, Boston.

Estabrook property deeds. Middlesex South Registry of Deeds. East Cambridge, Mass.

Journals of Each Provincial Congress of Massachusetts in 1774 and 1775 and the Committee of Safety. Boston: William Lincoln, 1837. Accounts taken shortly after April 19, 1775 from many Lexington militiamen who took part in the encounter on the Battle Green are reprinted in *The Journals of Each Provincial Congress of Massachusetts in 1774 and 1775 and of the Committee of Safety with an Appendix*, edited by William Lincoln, Boston, 1838.

Lexington Assessors Office. Lexington Assessors Records, 1780–1805. Lexington, Mass.: Town Office Building.

Lexington, Massachusetts. *Record of Births, Marriages, and Deaths to January 1, 1898*. Boston: 1898.

Manuscript Minutes of the Board of Selectmen, 1713 to 1840. Town Clerk's office. Transcript in Lexington Historical Society archives.

Massachusetts Heads of Families, First Census of the United States, 1790, Microfilm publication, M637, roll 4. National Archives, Northeast Region, Waltham, Mass.

Massachusetts Soldiers and Sailors of the Revolutionary War. Records compiled from the archives by the Secretary of the Commonwealth, Boston: 1899. Copies in Cary Memorial and other libraries.

Muster rolls of the Revolution, state militia, Massachusetts Archives Collection, File F, Vol. 55, p. 50.

Records of Littleton, Massachusetts, Births and deaths from the earliest records in the town books. Littleton, Mass.: 1900.

Revolutionary War military records, including muster rolls, Microfilm publication M-246 Revolutionary War Rolls, 1775–1783. National Archives, Northeast Region, Waltham, Mass.

Revolutionary War Pension and Bounty Land Warrant application files, 1800–1900, Microfilm publication M-804, 2670 rolls. National Archives, Northeast Region, Waltham, Mass.

Vital Records of Bedford, to the year 1850. Boston: New England Historic Genealogical Society, 1903.

Local histories

Brown, Abram English. *History of the Town of Bedford, Massachusetts from Its Earliest Settlement to the Year of Our Lord, 1891*. Bedford, Mass.: Bedford Free Library Corp., 1976.

Brown, Louise K. *A Revolutionary Town*. Canaan, N.H.: Phoenix Publishers, 1975. Published in cooperation with the Bedford Historical Society.

Bryant, Albert W. "The Military Organizations of Lexington." *Proceedings of the Lexington Historical Society*, Vol. 11, 1890–1899. Read Dec. 9, 1890.

Cutter, Benjamin and William R. *History of the Town of Arlington*. Boston: David Clapp, 1880.

Drake, Samuel. *History of Middlesex County, Massachusetts*. Boston: 1897.

Fuess, Claude M. *Andover: Symbol of New England*. Andover, Mass.: The Andover Historical Society and the North Andover Historical Society, 1959.

Hodgman, Rev. A.M. *History, Town of Westford 1659–1883*. Lowell, Mass.: The Westford Town History Association, 1883.

Hudson, Charles. *History of the Town of Lexington from its First Settlement to 1868, Vols. I and II*. Boston: Houghton Mifflin, 1913.

Hudson, Charles, *History of the Town of Lexington*. Vol. I with genealogies, 1886.

Hurd, D.H., *The History of Middlesex County, Mass.*, Vol. 2. Philedelphia: JW and Co., 1890.

Kidder and Gould. *History of New Ipswich from First Grant in MDCCXXXVI to the Present Time*. Boston: 1852.

MacLean, John C. *A Rich Harvest, The History, Buildings and People of Lincoln, Massachusetts*. Lincoln, Mass.: Lincoln Historical Society, 1987.

Paquet, Donat H. *The Photographic History of Dracut, Massachusetts*. Dracut, Mass.: Dracut Historical Society, Inc., 1982.

Parker, Charles Symmes. *Town of Arlington, Past and Present, 1637–1907*. Arlington, Mass.: C. S. Parker Sons, 1907.

Parker, Elizabeth S. "Captain John Parker." *Proceedings Lexington Historical Society*, vol. 1. Read Dec. 14, 1886.

Richardson, Eleanor Motley. *Andover: A Century of Change, 1886–1986*. Andover, Mass.: The Andover Historical Society, 1995.

Staples, Rev. C. A. "The Existence and Extinction of Slavery in Massachusetts." 1902 paper by the pastor, First Parish Unitarian Church Lexington from 1881–1904 and Lexington Historical Society historian. *Proceedings of the Lexington Historical Society*, Vol. IV, 1912.

Staples, Rev. C. A. "A Sketch of the History of Lexington Common." Read Oct. 12, 1886, *Proceedings of the Lexington Historical Society*, Vol. I, 1890.

Temple Josiah. *History of Framingham*, *Mass. 1640–1885*. A special centennial-year reprinting of the 1887 edition. New England History Press in collaboration with the Framingham Historical and Natural History Society, 1988.

Washburn, Emory. *Historical Sketches, Town of Leicester, Massachusetts*. Boston: John Wilson and Son, 1860,

"Washington's Dinner at Munroe Tavern." *Proceedings of the Lexington Historical Society*, Vol. 1. 1890.

Worthen, Edwin B. *A Calendar History of Lexington, Massachusetts, 1620–1946*. Lexington, Mass.: The Lexington Savings Bank, 1946.

Worthen, Edwin B. *Tracing the Past in Lexington, Massachusetts*. Edited by Anita Worthen. New York: Vantage Press, 1998.

Other books

Aptheker, Herbert. *A Documentary History of the Negro People in the United States*. New York: Citadel Press, 1951.

Bell, Edward. *Slaves in the Family*. New York: Ballantine Books, 1998.

Boatner, Mark M. *Encyclopaedia of the American Revolution*. New York: D. McKay Co., 1966.

Bolton, Charles Knowles. *The Private Soldier Under Washington*. New York: Charles Scribner's Sons, 1902.

Bray, Robert C. and Paul E. Bushnell, eds. *Diary of a Common Soldier in the American Revolution, 1775–1783: An Annotated Edition of the Military Jounal of Jeremiah Greenman*. DeKalb, Ill.: Northern Illinois University Press, 1978.

Calloway, Colin G. *The American Revolution in Indian Country*. Cambridge, England: Cambridge University Press, 1995.

Coburn, Frank Warren. *The Battle of April 19th, 1775*. Lexington, Mass.: 1912; revised, 1922. Published by the author.

Crevecoeur, J. Hector St. John. *Letters from an American Farmer*. Reprinted from the original. New York: Fox Duffield & Co., 1904.

David, Jay and Elaine Crane. *The Black Soldier: From the American Revolution to Vietnam*. New York: William Morrow Co., 1971.

Diamant, Lincoln. *Chaining the Hudson*. New York: Carol Publishing Group, 1989.

Dorman, Franklin A. *Twenty Families of Color in Massachusetts, 1742–1998*. Boston: New England Historic and Geneological Society, 1998.

Falkner, Leonard. *Forge of Liberty*. New York: Dutton, 1959.

Fischer, David Hackett. *Paul Revere's Ride*. New York: Oxford University Press, 1994.

Fishel, Leslie H. Jr. and Benjamin Quarles. *The Negro American*. Glenview, Ill.: Scott, Foresman and Co., 1967.

Fleming, Thomas. *Liberty! The American Revolution*. New York: Viking Penquin, 1977.

French, Allen. *The Day of Concord and Lexington: The Nineteenth of April, 1775*. Boston: Little, Brown & Co., 1925.

Frey, Sylvia R. *Water from the Rock, Black Resistance in a Revolutionary Age*. Princeton, N.J.: Princeton U Press, 1991.

Frothingham, Richard Jr., *History of the Seige of Boston, and the Battles of Lexington, Concord, and Bunker Hill*. Boston: 1851.

Galvin, Gen. John R. *The Minute Men*. The Association of the United States Army (AUSA), The Institute of Land Warfare Association of the US Army, 1989.

Garrison, William Lloyd. *The Loyalty and Devotion of Colored Americans in the Revolution and War of 1812*. Boston: 1851.

Greene, Lorenzo Johnson, Ph.D. *The Negro in Colonial New England 1620–1776*. New York: Columbia University Press, 1942.

Greene, Robert Ewell. *Black Courage 1775–1783*. Washington, D.C.: National Society of the Daughters of the American Revolution, 1984.

Gross, Robert A. *The Minutemen and Their World*. New York: Hill and Wang, 1976.

Hamilton, P. Edward. *Fort Ticonderoga, Key to the Continent*. Boston: Little Brown and Co., 1964. Amherst: University of Massachusetts Press, 1989. Revised edition.

Horton, James Oliver and Lois E. *In Hope of Liberty*. New York: Oxford University Press, 1997.

Howard, Rev. R. H. and Prof. Henry E. Crocker, eds. *A History of New England.* (Boston: Crocker & Co., 1881).

Kaplan, Sidney and Emma Nogrady Kaplan. *The Black Presence in the Era of the American Revolution, 1770–1800*. Amherst: U Massachusetts Press, 1989.

Katcher, Philip. *Uniforms of the Continental Army*. York, Pa.: George Shumway, 1981.

Larkin, Jack. *The Reshaping of Everyday Life, 1790–1840*. New York: Harper & Row, 1989.

Livermore, George. Read by Livermore before the Massachusetts Historical Society, Aug. 14, 1862. *Historical Research Respecting the Opinions of the Founders of the Republic on Negroes as Slaves, as Citizens, and as Soldiers*. Boston: A. Williams and Co., 1863.

Murdock, Harold. *The Nineteenth of April 1775*. Boston: Houghton Mifflin Co., 1925.

Muzzey, A.B. *The Battle of Lexington, with Personal Recollections of Men Engaged in It*. Boston: Walker, Wise and Co., 1877.

Nash, Gary. *Race and Revolution*. Madison, Wisc.: Madison House, 1990.

Nell, William C. *The Colored Patriots of the American Revolution*. New York: Arno Press and *The New York Times*, 1968

Newmann, George C. *Collectors Illustrated Encyclopedia of the American Revolution*. Harrisburg, Pa.: Stackpole Books, 1975.

Phinney, Elias. *History of the Battle at Lexington on the Morning of the 19th April, 1775*. Boston: Phelps and Farnham, 1825.

Powell, Colin, with Joseph E. Persico. *My American Journey*. New York: Ballantine Books, 1995.

Quarles, Benjamin. *The Negro in the American Revolution*. Williamsburg, Va.: University of No. Carolina Press, 1961.

Ripley, Ezra. *A History of the Fight at Concord on the 19th of April, 1775*. Concord, Mass.: Allen & Atwell, 1827.

Swett, Samuel. *Notes to His Sketch of Bunker-Hill Battle*. Boston: 1825.

Taylor, Robert J., ed. *Papers of John Adams, Vol. 3*. Cambridge, Mass.:Belknap Press, 1979.

Torrey, Bradford and Francis H. Allen, eds. *The Journals of Henry D. Thoreau*, Vols. VIII-XIV (November 1855–1861). New York: Dover Publications, 1962.

Tourtellot, Arthur B. *Lexington and Concord—The Beginning of the War of the American Revolution*. New York: W.W. Norton & Co., 1963.

Trevelyan, Sir George Otto. *The American Revolution, Part 1*. New York: Longmans, Green and Co., 1899.

Wright, Donald R. *African Americans in the Colonial Era*. Arlington Heights, Ill.: Harlan Davidson, Inc., 1990.

Wright, Robert K. Jr. *The Continental Army*. Washington, D.C.: Center of Military History, U.S. Army, 1989.

Zilversmit, Arthur. *The First Emancipation: The Abolition of Slavery in the North*. Chicago.: University of Chicago Press, 1967.

Unpublished papers, newspaper articles, and other materials

Canavan, M. J. Unpublished papers. Lexington, Mass.: Lexington Room, Cary Memorial Library (three volumes).

Edwin B. Worthen Collection. Lexington, Mass.: Cary Memorial Library.

Edmund Munroe letters. Lexington, Mass.: Lexington Historical Society archives.

Fitchburg Sentinel. Sept. 12, 1930 edition.

Griffin, Jay B., president of Medford Historical Society, "Prince Hall, A Man of Courage and Vision in Colonial Medford." Medford, Mass.: Part of city records, City Clerk's Office, 1992.

Massachusetts Society of the Sons of the American Revolution (SAR) bulletin. Nov. 1930.

Mayo, Martha. Research for *Profiles in Courage Exhibit, African Americans in Lowell.* Center for Lowell History, Lowell, Mass.

Minute Man National Historical Park pamphlet. Information on park and Battle Road Trail. 1991.

Parker, Captain John. Deposition on events, April 19, 1775. Lexington Historical Society archives.

Photographic Collection of the New England Society for the Preservation of Antiquities. Boston.

Pompey Blackman letter. Papers of Amos Fortune. Jaffrey, N.H. Public Library archives.

Powell, Colin. Speech in Ft. Leavenworth, Kans., at the dedication of the Buffalo Soldier Monument, July 25, 1992.

Robertson, Tatsha. "Echoes of the Underground Railroad." Article in *The Boston Globe*, Feb. 22, 1999.

Rufus Merriam psalm book. Lexington, Mass.: Lexington Historical Society archives.

Ryan, D. Michael, Concord Minute Men historian. "Slavery and Two fights for Freedom." Article in *Concord Journal*, Aug. 8, 1996, p. 16.

Sabin, Douglas P. "April 19, 1775: A Historiographical Study." Sabin is a retired staff historian at Minute Man National Historical Park. Concord, Mass.: 1987.

Sabin, Douglas P. "The Role of Blacks in the Battle of April 19, 1775." Minute Man National Historical Park publication, circa 1992.

Tolman, George. *John Jack, the Slave, and Daniel Bliss, the Tory.* Pamphlet in Concord Free Public Library Special Collections, Concord, Mass.: 1902.

Trumbull, Joan. "Concord and the Negro." Paper, March 16, 1944, Concord Free Public Library Special Collections.

Wallace, Teresa. Curator, Minute Man National Historical Park, Peter Salem paper. Concord, Mass.: June 2000.

Acknowledgments

Very special thanks to modern-day Lexington Minute Man Charles Price, who keeps the spirit of Prince Estabrook alive by his moving portrayal of this slave and soldier in reenactments on Lexington's Battle Green. Price, pictured on the front cover, spent countless hours sharing his thoughts on Estabrook's role: what it may have meant in 1775, what it means to him, and what it might mean to us today. His comments and insights helped shape this story.

Lexington historian and Battle Green guide director S. Lawrence Whipple fueled my interest in local history, offering wit and wisdom, facts and leads, and photos from his collection. Lexington Historical Society executive director George Comtois made it as easy as possible to examine the society's files. He also rediscovered an eighteenth-century psalm book with a direct link to Estabrook.

Richard McCarthy, Irma Catallini, Ken Johnson, and others in Ashby, Mass., gave tips and information, even a tour of a former Estabrook family home. Harvey Bakari, manager of African-American programs at Colonial Williamsburg, Wayne Smith, past president of the Black Patriots Foundation in Washington, D.C., and Mark Gresham, current foundation president, shared information on the efforts these organizations are making to honor Revolutionary War soldiers of color.

Minute Man National Historical Park superintendent Nancy Nelson, curator Teresa Wallace, chief of interpretation Lou Sideris, and park ranger Mark Nichipor were generous with time, information, and the sharing of illustrations. Former Menotomy Minute Man captain Paul Hogman, Lexington Historical Society president and Lexington Minute Man Gardner "Skip" Hayward Jr., and Lexington Minute Man George Gabriel helped fill in details. Lexington Minute Man Alex Cain shared his research on a regiment in which Estabrook served. Costume historian Henry Cooke IV helped by delving into his vast knowledge of Revolutionary War uniforms and related items. Reenactor and Concord Minute Men historian D. Michael Ryan offered helpful comments and corrections, as did historian George Quintal and Arlington Historical Society museum consultant Lisa Welter.

Alan Amoine, senior special collections librarian at the U. S. Military Academy Library, provided background on Revolutionary War conditions in the Hudson Highlands, and Christopher Fox, Fort Ticonderoga Museum curator, added details about Fort Ticonderoga. Many community historians helped flesh out stories of other patriots of color and were key sources of facts, leads, and directions to important sites.

I'm grateful to friend and author Andrea Cleghorn for her unflagging encouragement and ideas dispensed over coffee, and for her thoughtful comments; to naturalist and author Tom Sileo for his assistance and passion for uncovering the layers of history around us; to historian and author David Hackett Fischer for the new insights into the familiar story of April 19th, 1775, in his "Paul Revere's Ride," and for his advice, suggestions, and interest in this project.

Thanks to the staff of the Museum of Our National Heritage, the Lowell Lecture Series, the *Boston Globe*, and the *Lexington Minuteman* newspapers for allowing me to bring earlier pieces of Prince Estabrook's story to the public. I appreciate the time taken by librarians at the Concord Free Public Library Special Collections' section, Arlington's Robbins Library, and the Andover Memorial Hall Library. The crew at Lexington's Cary Memorial Library, especially recently retired Julie Triessl, deserves special mention for helping me mine the library's treasures. They also connected me with Raymond Estabrook. This descendant of Joseph Estabrook II discovered that his family once held slaves when he came across Prince's name in Estabrook family histories. Our discussions added a new dimension to the story.

I am indebted to Ann Ringwood for her expressive cover shot of Charles Price; to Melissa Cook, whose editing helped keep me on track; to Jan van Steenwijk, the talented graphic designer, photographer, and history buff who poured enthusiasm and skill into the book's design, came up with its title, and lent support; to Jeanette Webb for her expertise and her thoughtful attention in preparing the book for publication; to John Dodge, who provided a critical illustration; to journalist Susan Fisher and Lexington Historical Society volunteer Jean Gavin for filling in gaps; and to scores of others who offered information, ideas, and their valuable time to help tell Prince's story.

I will always appreciate the many lessons I've learned from editors and colleagues and the patience of family and friends as my work turned from pastime to obsession. My husband, Bill, has listened, joined Estabrook expeditions, and has never complained about sharing me with Prince. Our sons—David, Tim, Chris, and Bob—gave me an early excuse to visit historical sites and encouraged my writing. They and their wives—Carolann, Margaret, Bethanne, and Meghan—offered welcome comments. Our grandchildren's excitement about minutemen, Redcoats, and Battle Road events is a hopeful sign that this story hasn't lost its appeal.

Finally, I want to thank the groups that helped support this project: the Lexington Council for the Arts, a local agency; the Massachusetts Cultural Council, a state agency; as well as the National Endowment for the Arts; and to the 1999 Dan H. Fenn/Lexington Minute Man Grant award, earmarked for the book's design and graphics.

A.M.H.

Illustration credits

Index

About this book

A portion of the proceeds from the sale of this book will support research on patriots of color and projects that foster awareness of these largely forgotten Revolutionary soldiers.

Alice Hinkle is a freelance journalist who lives a stone's throw from the Battle Road in Lexington, Mass. A correspondent for the *Boston Globe* and former editor of the *Lexington Minuteman* newspaper, Hinkle coauthored *A Lexington Sampler for Children*, and *Life in Lexington 1946–1995*. Patriot's Day is one of the favorite holidays of the Hinkle family, which includes Alice, her husband, Bill, and their four grown sons and their families.

Charles H. Price Jr. is a member and past commander of the modern-day Lexington Minute Men. After serving in the Korean War, Price earned a master of science degree and worked as an electrical engineer. Now, semiretired, he teaches at his alma mater, Northeastern University, in Boston. Price and his wife, Imelda, moved to Lexington in 1964, where they raised their three daughters, Cecelia, Carolyn, and Constance.

Jan van Steenwijk is a graphic designer and professional photographer who got hooked on American history after moving to this country from Holland and Denmark. Van Steenwijk heads Design Photo, in Bedford, Mass.; he and his wife, Barbara Hitchcock, collaborated to create the 1998 book, *The Bedford Flag: A National Treasure*.